MIDGET CAR SPEEDWAY

FOLLOWING THE FORTUNES OF STOKE POTTERS

MIDGET CAR SPEEDWAY

FOLLOWING THE FORTUNES OF STOKE POTTERS

DEREK BRIDGETT

TEMPUS

To Teddy and Harold

First published 2006

Tempus Publishing Limited
The Mill, Brimscombe Port,
Stroud, Gloucestershire, GL5 2QG
www.tempus-publishing.com

British Library Cataloguing in Publication Data.
A catalogue record for this book is available from the British Library.

ISBN 0 7524 3870 0

Typesetting and origination by Tempus Publishing Limited.
Printed in Great Britain.

Contents

Introduction

It was by chance that I stumbled across a long-lost programme for the opening meeting of Hanley Car Speedway for 21 July 1938. It was this discovery that began my interest in pre-war midget car racing. This programme and others had been hidden away amongst family papers for years. When it surfaced I remembered as a child my two older brothers often talking to me of the car racing they had witnessed at Hanley's Sun Street Stadium. At about the same time that the programmes surfaced, I attended the opening meeting at Rockingham Motor Speedway. On display there was a collection of midget cars from the past.

Knowing very little about this dynamic form of motor racing I set out to find out more. Little or nothing has been recorded about this short-lived form of motor sport. I hope that this introduction will change all that and encourage others to delve into midget car history, where they can search out forgotten articles, photographs and programmes and record them for posterity.

This book is by no means a definitive history of the sport but it follows events that lead to motor racing coming to The Potteries i.e. the city of Stoke-on-Trent. By concentrating on the race meetings that took place in Stoke, the reader will be able to build up a picture as to how the sport developed and prospered. Other tracks around the country are covered but by concentrating on one track in depth, a better picture will emerge rather than taking a more shallow overview of the 1938 and 1939 season.

one

An Idea
Takes Shape

In 1939, the headlines 'Car Racing at Cobridge' once appeared in the pages of a provincial evening newspaper. Motor racing historians seeing this caption might be seen scurrying for reference books and copies of old motor racing magazines, searching to find out where the Cobridge track was or to see if such an event took place. To the people of the Potteries, if such a headline were to appear today, they would think that it was the local petrol heads holding one of their illegal cruises, thrashing their customised cars around the car parks of the retail and leisure complex at Festival Park. Both would hardly believe that the sport of motor racing took place at Cobridge before the war; because Cobridge is a small urban parish between the towns of Hanley and Burslem in the city of Stoke-on-Trent. It is more famous as the birthplace of Arnold Bennett, whose novels based around the six towns of the Potteries received literal acclaim and success at the beginning of the twentieth century. Cobridge also boasts the famous Moorcroft Pottery factory, which is noted throughout the world for its Majolica ware pottery. Motor racing would hardly seem to fit into this environment and yet before the war, both Cobridge and nearby Shelton were to witness spectacular and exciting motor racing. For the little known – nor discussed – motor sport of midget car speedway took place at Sun Street Greyhound Stadium, Shelton in 1938 and briefly at the Albion Greyhound Stadium Cobridge during 1939. It is claimed that the first organised midget car meeting took place in June 1933 at Sacramento, California, before spreading to other parts of the United States, reaching Australia and the UK a couple of years later. This is not to say that racing cars around small oval circuits of around a quarter of a mile did not exist before this time. In this country, as elsewhere, such events were already taking place on short-circuit dirt ovals. It was the small purpose-built cars that were new; they were hand-built, using parts from cars, boats, motorcycles and anything else that would make the cars move. Many of the drivers were young men who had little or no experience of auto racing. Within a few years midget car racing would become the most popular sport in the USA with drivers being able to race four to seven nights a week. When the sport reached the Chicago region of the US, the reporter H.B. Overstreet, who was covering that area in January 1935, coined the phrase 'Doodle Bug', a term that was to stick almost throughout the entire history of the sport. As is well known, this term was later used to describe the German V1 flying bombs of the Second World War.

Before the Second World War motor racing was the preserve of the higher members of the socio-economic groups in society. Drivers were likely to come from the professions and the more well-off classes rather than car mechanics, garage owners, electricians and other artisans. Spectators too liked to think of themselves as a cut above the rest, the often quoted motto of the Brooklands race track, 'The Right Crowd and no Crowding' was the perfect way to sum up the pre-war motor racing scene. The post-war period was to see all that change as motor racing began to appeal to all members of society. It could be argued that these changes were taking place before the war and, although they might not know it at the time, the motor sport fans of the Potteries were at the forefront of this change. Midget car speedway enabled everybody and anybody to attend motor car racing. For in 1938 and 1939, car racing fans could stand shoulder to shoulder on the terraces of stadiums and watch single-seater racing cars driven flat

These cars were some of the very first midgets to be constructed in Australia. Ted Day, No. 19, leads Arthur Tuckett and George Beavis, No. 4.

out for four or more hectic laps around loose-surfaced ovals. These short sprints packed into them all the necessary skills and spills to keep an appreciative crowd entertained. This was a different form of motor racing, a gladiatorial contest that anybody could keep pace with, there was no need for stopwatches, lap charts, etc. The crowd could see all the action unfold in front of them. Concentrating on who was leading and who was where was unnecessary; this was motor racing with a populist appeal. When the first of the 'modern' midgets appeared at Belle Vue, Manchester, in 1936 the *Manchester Guardian* wrote,'…the new American midget cars were seen in action for the first time. They were a great improvement on anything previously tested at Belle Vue. Six of them brightly coloured and with sparks and flames spitting from the exhaust proved a good spectacle and they are certainly noisy enough to please the most hardened of Speedway Fans'. As can be seen from this extract the majority of the spectators were to be found amongst the already large following of motorcycle speedway fans. Stadiums that presented this new sport were situated in large towns and cities and were within easy reach of the populace. Public transport was specially laid on. Bus and train services were able to cope with the large influx of spectators. With the exception of London's Crystal Palace motor racing circuit, midget car speedway brought motor racing to the people, where previously the public had to travel out of town to the few venues that presented motor racing. Tradition has it that in February 1928 at High Beech in Epping Forest the first motorcycle speedway event took place in this country. Within a few months this new sport of 'dirt-track racing' – which had been introduced from Australia – swept the country. Such was the rapid expansion of this type of racing that by the end of that year, the governing body of motorcycle racing – The Auto Cycle Union (ACU) – had issued licences to at least thirty-four tracks. Seeing how well this new form of racing was going, it would not be long before the racing car fraternity decided they too would like to venture out on to the dirt track ovals.

Four months later, on Saturday 23 June, the first organised event took place at the half-mile Greenford Trotting Track near Ealing. At the time, neither of these motorised sports was taken too seriously. Competition, it was claimed, 'improved the breed'; pushing cars and motorcycles to their limits highlighted faults so that improvements could be incorporated into production vehicles. From the start of dirt-track racing it was argued that there was nothing in this pastime to aid

The first advertisement for short circuit oval racing that appeared in *Light Car and Cyclecar* magazine of 22 June 1928.

Frank Varey tries one of the new Elto midget cars for size.

Alan Kilfoyle's special that incorporated a rollover bar for driver safety.

development and was in fact described by the magazine *Light Car and Cyclecar* as 'circus work'. The same magazine also warned members of the public who might be going along purely to satisfy their craving to see crashes and spills, to stay away. They claimed that to fall from a motorcycle is one thing but to have a crash with a car is something entirely different. They encouraged their readers to regard the meeting 'as speed trials run under the most difficult conditions possible and scoring over the ordinary kind of speed trial in that progress of the race can be watched at comparatively close quarters from start to finish. If the public will take this sensible and moderate view of dirt-track racing for cars there may be a future for the sport'. The die had been cast; racing cars and bikes around loose-surfaced ovals in the confines of stadiums was not 'proper' motor sport; a view that still pervades in some quarters today. The motoring press were unsure as what to call this new form of racing: and for a while the term 'Dracing' was used; possibly a shortened version of dirt-track racing.

This first event was organised, not by those professional showmen who had put on the first motorbike events but by one of the foremost motoring organisations of the time: The Junior Car Club, who had been responsible for several prestigious events at the Brooklands Circuit. The admittance charge for spectators ranged from 1s 6d (7.5p) to a rather expensive 7s 6d (37.5p). The rather high entrance fee would have discouraged the ordinary 'man in the street'.

Races were split into classes and competed three cars to a race. There was also one major difference between the bikes and the cars, in so much as the cars were to race in a clockwise direction as opposed to the anti-clockwise direction of the motorbikes. It was claimed that the reason for this was that because the cars were right-hand drive, the weight of the driver was on the inside and made for safer cornering.

The first meeting duly went ahead with a collection of various sports cars and suitable single-seater racing cars, the best of which proved to be those cars – both sports and single seaters – from the workshops of the Frazer-Nash company. A.G.F. Nash in his single seater was the best driver–car combination on the day. In what was loosely described as the best 'final' of the day, he won at an average speed of 44.12mph. The attendance at this meeting was nowhere near the attendance figures for the motorcycle speedway event at the White City Stadium, London, where a crowd of over 78,000 was reported. The cars couldn't compete with the bikes, attendance wise, and the two sports went their separate ways. The bike riders were highly paid; the top riders were among the highest paid sportsmen in inter-war Britain. Frank Varey, a top Belle Vue rider – who was to try his hand briefly with midget cars – recalled that 'we were the ones going round in flash cars, not the footballers'. Rider's equipment, too, was becoming even more professional; most motorcycle manufacturers now carried a speedway bike in their catalogue of machines for sale. Not so the cars, which remained very much amateur and fun. Over the next two years one or two tentative steps were taken to stage dirt-track racing for cars. In late 1929 the sport was introduced to the Midlands. In November a one-third-of-a-mile track was built inside the Leicester Super Stadium. Again the cars were the usual sports and single seaters. The star of the show was Brayston driving an Alvis. For the few spectators that attended the meeting they could only hope that forth-coming events would get better. In what was claimed to be the best race of the afternoon, only two cars competed, A. Burnham in a Salmson and O. Bentley in an Amilcar, who passed and re-passed in one of the semi-finals of the scratch races. The reporter at the meeting said that with only two cars in the race it gave drivers much more room to manoeuvre. He also noted that the man who took the inside during the rolling start had a great advantage.

For the sport to develop and improve, specialist cars were needed, especially at this time, when cars were beginning to compete on the purpose-built speedway tracks. These smaller tracks needed a fresh approach. Alan Kilfoyle a well-known speedway rider of the time was just one such specialist builder. He constructed a car he hoped would be successful on the speedway tracks. His car was an interesting attempt. At the car's first trials the radius arms on the front axle snapped, thus highlighting the different stresses put on the chassis when the car broadsided around the tight bends.

two

Tentative
Steps

The sport stuttered on for a couple of years and could have quite easily faded away. But news was drifting across the Atlantic of what was happening in the United States; and what was happening there was nothing short of a revolution. A revolution not only in motor racing terms, but also in car construction and most importantly spectator appeal. The news reports and newsreels coming out of the United States was mainly concerned with the Great Depression. Hidden amongst the dreary news, there was just a hint of optimism to lift the gloom. The revolution that was taking place was the new sport of midget car racing. This new sport exploded on to the US motor sport scene and was to imbed itself into the mainstream of American culture. Oval racing in the US had a fabulous heritage; there were not only the paved ovals and dirt tracks but there had also been the fantastically fast board tracks, many of which were now in a state of disrepair and were now defunct. The difference between this new form of oval racing and the old form was the cars and circuits. The older ovals were expensive to run and maintain, as were the cars. The new smaller tracks and cars struck a chord; there was something different, a fresh start, a new deal for motor racing, and an escape from the Depression.

It was only thirteen days after the first successful meeting at Sacramento that the action moved to Baxter Stadium, Stockton, CA. Then the excitement spread 400 miles southwards along the coast to arrive at Loyola Stadium, Los Angeles, in August. Here they were an instant success; there were large crowds culled from the large population base around the LA area. But above all, there were a more reasonable number of cars competing. Here in California, midget car racing gained a foot hold, a springboard to spread to other parts of the country. This state was well placed to see the gestation of midget car racing. Despite the uncertainty of the economy, the West Coast had everything going for it. With the film industry based there they were well able to sell dreams. The midget car promoters were able to learn from the movie publicists and were able to aggressively sell their new product to the receptive populace.

There were also several skilled engineers working in the area who could produce the necessary components for race car manufacture. These engineers formed a sound basis and had a strong tradition of making parts for motor racing. Within a very short space of time West Coast speed shops had produced professional, well-made, pretty little cars with lots of chrome and stunning paint jobs. Before the midgets reached this high standard the cars went through a rather intense evolutionary process. As there was nothing for the amateur constructors to refer to, cars just seemed to evolve naturally. Some of the early cars had been nothing short of jalopies with smoky, unreliable engines gleaned from all sorts of sources. Some of these early cars were even street legal with a few drivers dispensing with transporters and driving their cars to meetings.

One fascinating car–driver combination that appeared at Loyola on 10 August 1933 was Bill Battenridge. Bill had built his little racer from bits and pieces lying around his father's garage. He had finished constructing his car in late December 1932, having built it not to any set of rules or preconceived ideas, but purely for his own enjoyment. What he had put together was a scaled-down version of the cars he had seen at the famed Legion Ascot track in Los Angeles. As midget racing took hold and cars improved, so Bill developed his 'Little Red Racer'. His car

A typical special that raced on the US ovals of the late 1920s and early 1930s.

Bill Battenridge stands proudly behind the midget car he constructed in his spare time. Sadly, Bill was to lose his life racing his midget car at Atlantic Speedway (LA) in June 1937.

had started out with a Henderson motorcycle engine, but later in 1934 the more powerful Elto engine replaced this. Once midgets had established a foothold in California some sort of organisation was needed. One of the guiding lights behind the early organisation of the sport was Ken Brennen of Oakland, CA. Not only did he build and race his own car but he also had enough drive to head the first sanctioning body. Like the founding fathers, some of the rules that they formulated back in 1933 are still relevant today; they still race with the same configuration and wheelbase.

It wasn't long before other centres decided to latch onto the new phenomena. As the name implies, midget cars didn't take up much room to race; venues to stage racing were plentiful. Every town with a baseball team or high school track had the potential to have a racetrack. The following year, 1934, tracks began opening nationwide, and racing had reached the Chicago area. The Blue Mound Road Dog Track at Milwaukee opened on 12 July and, significantly, Irvington, New Jersey, opened too. For it was in New Jersey, as a result of midget car racing, that a newspaper dedicated solely to presenting motor racing went into publication. For the first time a publication served the growing fan base around New Jersey, but even more significantly, the paper went nationwide. This paper, *The National Auto News*, flourished as the new fans of auto racing now found a way of keeping up with their favourite drivers. The top aces were now touring the country and racing at venues all around the US.

By 1935 every major city now staged midget car racing. The St Louis track opened in January. By the end of March there were tracks at Detroit's Fairground Coliseum, the Cleveland Equestrian Hall, Ohio, and the Indianapolis Coliseum, Indiana. Like an uncontrollable forest fire, midget car racing had spread to the Olympic Field, Kansas, then on to Omaha, Nebraska, New England and the Louisville Coliseum, Kentucky. Within less than two years midget car racing was now in every state of the Union. It would not be an exaggeration to say that with its simple rules and low cost, midget car racing had by then become one of the most significant innovations in motor racing history.

What was now needed in the UK was a complete re-think and re-vamp as how to present this exciting new product. Seeing that money could be made out of the presentation of car speedway, one or two speedway promoters started to look at how the sport might be developed. It was generally felt that because the sport was flourishing in the States it would only be a matter of time before it expanded in this country. Come 1934 and a fresh approach was taken. In May of that year Greenford was again the venue, this time the meeting was not presented by the J.C.C. but a new body known as The Autodrome Racing Club whose object was to develop this form of entertainment. One of the appointments that this club made was that of Technical Advisor. This post was filled by the inspirational Alvin 'Spike' Rhiando, a 'Canadian' opportunist who had landed on these shores with the intention of establishing car speedway racing. It was Spike who more or less organised and ran the whole event.

The sport was moving towards a more professional approach. There was also another difference between the 1934 event and the 1928 event, this time the cars raced in an anti-clockwise direction, and cars were to race this way for the rest of the midget car speedway era. There was the usual varied collection of cars competing, from

The flamboyant Spike Rhiando on the right with his mechanic.

the Conan Doyle's super-charged Mercedes down in size to a Le Mans Singer Nine, a J2 MG midget and several Ulster-type Austin Sevens. There was also a three-litre Bugatti that won two events at 56mph, considerably quicker than the 44.12mph of 1928.

One interesting novelty that took place at the Greenford meeting was nothing to do with the cars or the racing, but the attitude of the spectators when they began to applaud a particularly good dice or close race, this was something that had been unheard of in motor sport, and as one reporter of the time said, 'a strange thing at car races'.

A much more practical approach for the expansion of the sport took place earlier in the month when the Crystal Palace speedway track became available; this was because the 'Glaziers', Crystal Palace's speedway team, had moved to a new venue at New Cross. To record the change from two wheels to four; and to show the rest of the country what could be the start of something new, British Paramount Newsreel deemed it important enough to send along a film crew to record this first meeting for posterity. The quarter-mile oval should have been ideal for midget car speedway, but the problem was that there weren't any suitable midget cars, nor was there a definitive set of rules and regulations for race meetings and car design.

At Crystal Palace's early meetings the cars that dominated were the usual cut-down roadsters, particularly the Riley of Victor Gillow. But there were signs of change when Jean Revelle and Australian Tommy Sullman produced cars more suitable for the smaller speedway tracks. Car speedway was beginning to find its niche in motor sport. Apart from Greenford and Crystal Palace, events were tried at Dagenham and Lea Bridge, the later two were again ex-speedway tracks.

Left: Gene Revelle's B.S.A. engined Palmer Special, the gentleman standing next to him emphasising the size of the car.

Below: The small boy and the spare wheel, taken off a B.S.A. Scout, again showed the size and the direction Revelle wanted to take midget car construction.

The sport was now at a crossroad and politics began to rear its head. Several organisations appeared – two of which were more or less the same; these were The Midget Car Speedway Club and the Midget Car Speedway Association, both masterminded by Jean Revelle. Revelle created small cars that were about to be put on offer – this was a step in the right direction regarding car design.

In contrast to Revelle's organisation there was the London Car Speedway Club whose HQ was given as 142 Holland Park Avenue, W.1 and was inspired by Victor Gillow. It was the former that pushed forward; Gillow's association tended more towards the social aspect – and perhaps represented the more established side of motor racing. It was Revelle's association that was pushing the boundaries. They were the first to draw up rules as to how midget cars should be. Engine capacity was limited to 1,100cc, super-chargers were banned, wheelbase was to be no more than 5ft 6in, track not to exceed 3ft 6in, diameter of wheels not less than 12in and not more than 14in, beaded-edged tyres banned, brakes compulsory, tank to be made of 18-gauge material, ground clearance no less than 4in and finally the exhaust pipes were to extend beyond the back axle.

While the midget fraternity was battling for the heart and minds of those involved, there was, looming in the background, the National Speedway Association; these were the promoters that ran motorcycle speedway in this country. This band of entrepreneurs had been eyeing the progress of car speedway and many of them had used the cars as second-half attractions at their bike meetings. A conflict of interests was beginning to develop. Speedway promoters, being speedway promoters, wanted to exploit anything that would put 'bums on seats'. Using cars in the second half capitalised on the come-and-be-thrilled instincts of the man in the street. Another reason why promoters were looking at car speedway was because recent legislation had limited Greyhound meetings that could be held per week. As all the major speedway tracks bar one shared their stadia with greyhounds, stadium owners were always looking at ways of raising extra revenue. However the A.C.U. were firmly against cars sharing the same bill as bikes, and as they were the ones who held the 'trump cards', so to speak, they could revoke the licence of anyone who stepped out of line.

1934 and the year before that had been rather ignominious. However, it was in 1935 that the seeds were set that were to develop car speedway and see it germinate into the team racing of 1938 and the open meetings in 1939 that were to take place in Stoke-on-Trent. A formula for car design was in place and commercialisation through the use of sports stadiums was taking place. Now midget car speedway was starting to get its act together. The problem of not enough decent cars was about to be addressed. Jean Revelle Midget Cars Ltd had been set up – it was said with 'almost unlimited capital'! The company was hoping to manufacture fifty midgets by Easter of that year and hoping to build 150 cars in due course!

Rules and regulations were in force and the Midget Car Speedway Association had taken offices at 119 Bishops Gate, London, E.C. The organisation of meetings was improving; following the slick, well-run way that motorcycle speedway was presented. Team racing too, appeared for the first time. A team labelled 'England' met a team loosely described as the 'Continent' at Lea Bridge. There was also a best pairs championship. Most important of all, from a driver's point of view, was remuneration. Motorcycle speedway riders at the time were highly paid. It was felt in some quarters that car drivers racing around the same tracks in the same stadium should be paid the same. At Crystal Palace, drivers were paid £2 a race starting money. If a driver won every heat he would come away with another £14. An interesting form of payment was that used by The London Car Speedway Club at Lea Bridge whereby all the drivers had a share of 70 per cent of the total gate receipts. Interest was spreading. Over the Whitsuntide holiday of 1935 Londoners could have attended all midget car meetings at Crystal Palace, Lea Bridge and Catford.

The line up of 'midgets' for the first meeting at Manchester's Belle Vue Stadium, 1935.

Harry Skirrow with the first speedway car he constructed. At demonstration events he was introduced as 'The One Armed Lakeland Wonder'.

The manager of Belle Vue speedway stadium in Manchester began to see the potential of midget car speedway and was prepared to present an all-car meeting on 6 May. He invited, 'Anyone who has a real midget car and needs the opportunity of trying it out on the speedway had better come along to Belle Vue. We shall be pleased to give him every possible facility'. The meeting duly took place, but did not live up to the anticipated standard that the motorcycle speedway crowd were used to. The *Manchester Guardian*'s report on the meeting said, 'The Midget Car racing at Belle Vue Manchester last night proved a failure'. A poor start indeed. In fact expectations had been too high. Furthermore, the expected fifty cars that Jean Revelle was going to build never materialised. There was still hope for the sport; organisation was better and mechanical failure less. A further meeting held at Belle Vue in July was hailed a success, when on a wet night it was claimed 30,000 spectators turned up. This time a reporter in the *News Chronicle* said 'Midget motor-car racing on Manchester's Belle Vue speedway track has, in my opinion, come to stay'. As a result of these meetings, one person emerged who was to indelibly leave his mark on the sport and be forever associated with midget car racing. That person was Harry Skirrow. Having seen the cars and heeding the Belle Vue manager's invitation to special builders, he returned to his native Westmorland, constructed a car, took it to Belle Vue, and set in motion a chain of events that would see midget car racing reach all areas of England and beyond. Skirrow was not the only one with inventive and radical ideas about car construction. Dickie Case – one of the stars of the Hackney Wick speedway team

– built a rear-engined special. This he used in demonstrations at Hackney Wick and other London tracks. At the start of the year Jean Revelles' vision for the sport had looked encouraging and his enthusiasm for the sport continued with several different car designs until he finally settled for 'The Gnat'. At the end of the 1935 season, together with Ralph Sectarian and Bud Stanley, he took off for a tour of Australia. After a successful tour visiting most of the Australian tracks he decided to stay there where he competed successfully until retirement. The other two returned on the steamer RMS *Orsova* docking at Southampton in early 1936. This departure of Revelle left a void in midget car circles; this gap was more than adequately filled when finally towards the end of 1936, midget car speedway was put on a sound commercial footing, professionally presented and a viable spectator sport to match the well established spectacle of motorcycle speedway.

Midget cars were becoming a feature in second-half events at motorcycle speedway meetings. By now there were sufficient small cars and decent drivers. In August a full car meeting was staged at Hackney Wick with the grandiose title of World Championship! This was won by motorcycle star Cordy Milne who hailed from the USA.

It was speedway promoter Jim Baxter who tied up all the loose ends. He threw all his experience behind this new venture. He drew together like-minded promoters and enthusiasts. Between them they set up a new governing body. A fresh set of rules and regulations governing car dimensions and race procedure was introduced. This new body called itself The National Association of Speedway Car Racing Circuits. The new rules relating to car specifications were similar to the previous set. There was no mention of wheelbase, but chassis were not to exceed 6ft. Track was limited to 3ft 10in, engines were not to exceed 1,500cc and super-chargers were prohibited. Efficient brakes must be fitted, but this was a moot point; brakes that were fitted were operated by hand and were really of little use on the speedway tracks. The speedway bikes of the time had dispensed with brakes years before. Other rules governing car construction were merely cosmetic; 'A body shall be fitted to the

Gene Revelle in the 'Gnat' at Sydney Showground. (Courtesy of Gerry Baker, Australia)

Duel advert for Lea Bridge and Coventry 1937.

chassis of a single seater type'. No passengers were to be carried! 'All cars must be in racing trim. Only a windshield of an approved type may be fitted'. Finally there was one over-riding factor and that was 'every car entered in competition shall be subject to inspection by the N.A.S.C.R.C. representative before going on any track'. This last bit of legislation ensured that the promoters had a strangle hold on who did or did not drive. It was rather the same as the infamous 'spirit of Le Mans formula' that the Automobile Club de L'Ouest implements when accepting entries for their 24hour race.

With this new set of rules behind him, Jim Baxter introduced his version of the sport at tracks where there was no conflict of interests between cars and bikes. This allowed him to build up a regular support base for cars that could spread to other areas. A major problem and a serious headache had been suitable cars. In motorcycle speedway racing the bikes had now become more or less standardised. They all used the J.A.P. engine and it was only the frames that differed. Baxter solved the car problem with the help of Harry Skirrow, because Skirrow was about to make his latest car available to all. They became partners and formed the company 'Car Speedway Limited' which ran meetings in 1937 at Lea Bridge and Coventry; both these tracks no longer presenting bike racing. The other clubs and associations that had run car meetings faded away, the sport was now a hard-nosed business venture. There was little or no room for the enthusiastic amateur; those who now raced expected to be paid, just as the bike boys were (but I am sure that if some-one wanted to drive for nothing then the promoters would only be to happy to oblige!) Revenue to pay the drivers and stadium rental was generated solely through the number of spectators that passed through the turnstiles. Midget car speedway racing was now a serious business and about to take on motorcycle speedway racing and challenge other forms of motor sport to win over the support of the paying public.

three

League Racing is Introduced

The year 1938 was to be the season for midget car speedway. The previous year had shown that with the limited number of drivers available, team racing was the way forward. If exposed to a diet of individual events and novelty fixtures the paying public would soon tire. Jim Baxter, the driving force behind the midget car scene, pushed forward his desire for team events. He was following the same successful route that he had taken during the pioneering days of motorcycle speedway racing. Jim Baxter had been one of the early promoters of dirt-track racing; but most important of all he was one of the promoters behind the push for league racing. Once the novelty of seeing motorbikes 'Broadsiding' around the corners throwing up clouds of cinders had worn off. 'Joe Public' wanted more and team racing saved the day and proved to be the way forward. Baxter realised that spectators would remain loyal to a local team competing in a national or regional league and would be more likely to attend further meetings to cheer on their home side rather than follow individual drivers.

How then was this team racing to be achieved and where were the tracks to come from? Well there were eighteen teams operating in the two motorcycle speedway leagues, all suitable venues for midget car speedway. Also there were several stadiums that had once put on speedway meetings, of which one was Sun Street Stadium Hanley.

A pilot league had been tried the year before but this had been based on just two tracks: those at Brandon, near Coventry, and Lea Bridge, in London. Four teams competed; the Provinces and Coventry raced at Brandon, Lea Bridge and London raced at Lea Bridge. By early September that year the fixtures had been completed with the Provinces topping the table:

	Matches	Won	Lost	Points
Provinces	6	5	1	10
Coventry	6	4	2	8
Lea Bridge	6	3	3	6
London	6	1	5	2

This pilot league had been run along similar lines as motorcycle speedway. The newly-proposed National Car Speedway league was also to follow this familiar format. Matches were to be raced both home and away with a championship trophy at stake. Each team was to have six drivers a side plus a reserve; the teams would meet each other over twelve heats. Each heat would see two cars from each side competing over four laps. Three points were awarded to the winner, two for second, and one for third place. The side scoring the most points was declared the winner and was awarded two match points.

Lea Bridge and Coventry were by now well-established venues, both tracks running events purely for midget cars. Some speedway tracks (Southampton, Wembley, Norwich and Hackney Wick) had included cars in the second half of motorcycle speedway meetings as an added attraction. The White City Stadium at Ibrox, Glasgow, had run a series of meetings in May and June 1937. They had chosen to present midget car racing as team events. Their first two meetings had been the crowd-pleasing England v Scotland and Glasgow v Manchester matches. Because of the long trek up from England, English drivers were precluded from

Lea Bridge programme cover from 1937.

The no frills programme cover from Glasgow. (Courtesy of Ian Somerville)

further events. The Glaswegians needed to find a fresh approach to continue team racing. Their novel answer was to introduce three team tournaments. There were three drivers per race each representing his designated team. Novel names were chosen for the teams: Red Devils, Falcons, Grasshoppers and Titans, to name a few. Incidentally one of the teams was made up of Glasgow Corporation bus drivers. It may seem strange that someone with as mundane a job as a bus driver could afford to race a single-seater racing car in 1937. The answer to this was that the promoters owned the cars and these were loaned out to drivers that had showed promise at special trials. Unfortunately, racing ceased north of the border after just two months. But above all, there was one track that continued to keep faith with the little cars and that was Belle Vue, Manchester.

A handful of tracks scattered around the country were now available to form the nucleus of the league. The difficulty was trying to persuade the tracks that ran motorcycle speedway racing that car racing would be compatible with their operations and most important of all be financially rewarding. At the start of 1938 several tracks associated themselves with the formation of the league. At the opening event of the midget car season, held at Southampton on Good Friday, 15 April, it was expected that the league would consist of at least six teams. The six were Belle Vue, Coventry, Lea Bridge, Leicester, Southampton and Wembley. There was no mention of any team competing in the league from the Potteries. It was only a couple of months later that the name Stoke was mentioned as a possible starter in the league. The *News Chronicle* of 13 July intimated that apart from the aforementioned teams, Middlesbrough, Perry Bar (Birmingham) and possibly Stoke might join the league. Similarly two teams from Scotland notably those from Marine Gardens, Edinburgh and White City, Glasgow. Much of this optimism was unfounded. Typical of the promoters at that time, they were trying to maximise publicity by talking up their new venture. As ever, some promoters were making grandiose claims as to what they were doing and what they were going to do. This was not too bad a thing as it kept the public interest alive.

The majority of the tracks mentioned had had some connection with Jim Baxter. His company – Speedway Cars Ltd – whose directors were J. Baxter, H. Skirrow and E. Skirrow, ran the successful tracks at Coventry and Lea Bridge. Baxter's previous forays in motorcycle speedway promotion had been with several different associates. Tom Bradbury-Pratt, the director of Southampton, had previously co-promoted with Baxter at tracks in London. Bradbury-Pratt also controlled Middlesbrough and a few years previous had promoted at Birmingham. Wembley was under the direction of Arthur Elvin and in 1931, when Baxter was

One rider affected by the S.C.B. ban was international speedway star Bill Kitchen. Bill had won the opening midget car race at Belle Vue in 1936.

at West Ham and in financial difficulties, it was Elvin's management team that had taken over. Not all speedway promoters were keen to see midget cars on their tracks. Norwich had tried them as a second-half attraction. After a demonstration the Norwich management discovered how badly the cars cut up the track. They only appeared again at the very last meeting of 1937 when any damage to the track didn't matter. The speedway promoters were eager not to allow any of their riders to take up the four-wheeled version of their sport. In 1937, after plans had been announced to put midget car speedway on a sound commercial footing, the Speedway Control Board – i.e. the governing body of motorcycle speedway – reviewed the situation as to their riders taking part in midget car racing. They came up with the directive that speedway riders who were registered with the A.C.U. were permitted to drive in midget car meetings when these meetings were held on the tracks of the promoters who held their racing contracts. This, in effect, banned speedway riders from crossing over to race midget cars on other tracks. This concession still allowed the speedway promoters to put on midgets as a second-half attraction. It was not only the S.C.B. that was not very helpful but also the Speedway Press. The *Speedway News*, a publication that had an estimated circulation of around 25,000 copies per week, and was sold at the eighteen active speedway tracks around the country, was very anti-car. They claimed that their journal was devoted to motorcycle speedway and would not carry reports or gossip about car racing. Furthermore, they also refused to accept advertising from midget car promoters. They claimed that their readers would dislike trespass on their pages by an outside sport, however closely allied. Piously, they took the high moral ground by stating that midget car racing did not come under the supervision of the R.A.C. which, in their opinion, was the proper authority. Despite the anti-car lobby, two established motorcycle tracks wholeheartedly threw in their lot with the proposed midget car league. The two biggest names in speedway, Wembley and Belle Vue, were right behind this new venture. Perhaps this was because they were much bigger establishments than the other greyhound stadiums. Wembley and Belle Vue needed the extra revenue that car racing would generate. As early as 1935, when Belle Vue were encouraging hopeful car builders to bring along their creations, Mr Spence stated in *Light Car and Cyclecar* of 3 May that when suitable cars were found...'League racing would be a foregone conclusion'. As for Wembley, anything and everything was tried to fill the stadium. Being such huge enterprises, revenue from any source would be welcome.

During the winter of 1937/38 those parties interested in forwarding the aspirations of the midget car fraternity met to form a Board of Control to govern and conduct the general affairs of the sport. The National Car Speedway Association had already formulated rules and regulations. Everyone that had a financial stake in the sport joined the Board. The eight members who made up the Board were well known speedway personalities whose intentions were to maximise, through their joint efforts, the profitability of the sport. The eight who were to control the sport were: Mr E.O. Spence of Belle Vue; Tom Bradbury-Pratt and Charles Knott, both of Southampton; Alex Jackson, the Wembley team manager; Jim Baxter, promoter of both Lea Bridge and Coventry; Ron Hewitt, who had been a Steward with the National Car Speedway Association the previous year and was negotiating to run car speedway at Leicester; Harry Skirrow, manufacturer of the Skirrow

LEA BRIDGE CAR SPEEDWAY

LEA BRIDGE ROAD, LEYTON, E.10

LONDON'S FIRST SPEEDWAY CAR LEAGUE MATCH

On Wednesday, June 22nd, at 8.15 p.m.

LEA BRIDGE v. COVENTRY

SPIKE RHIANDO (Capt.)	WALTER MACKERETH (Capt.)
BASIL DE MATTOS	GEORGE TURVEY
STAN MILLS	FRANK CHISWELL
FRANK BULLOCK	JOHNNY YOUNG
JIMMY RAYNES	BUSTER BLADEN
TONY HUME	VAL ATKINSON

IN TWELVE GREAT HEATS

Also Another Sensational LONG DISTANCE RACE

AND FULL SUPPORTING PROGRAMME

GO DOODLE-DICING AND BE THRILLED!

NEXT WEEK :-

WEDNESDAY, JUNE 29th at 8.15 p.m.

Another League Clash :

LEA BRIDGE v. BELLE VUE

Admission 1s., 1s. 6d., and 2s.   Children 6d.   ● Car Park   ● Refreshments

SPIKE RHIANDO

WALTER MACKERETH

JIMMY RAYNES

GEORGE TURVEY

Ten days after the first league match, Coventry won again, this time at Lea Bridge.

Special and co-promoter with Jim Baxter at Lea Bridge and Coventry and, finally, Victor Martin who was connected with J.A. Prestwich, the engine manufacturer. The affairs of the Board were to be conducted from offices at Buchanan House in London's Holborn district. It was from these offices that Guy Hopkins was employed as a full-time secretary. Guy Hopkins was a respected motoring journalist whose column in *Speed* magazine kept midget car race fans well abreast of the latest news. His duties included processing applications and issuing racing licences to the drivers. He also acted as a general Public Relations Officer, writing many programme notes for tracks around the country. Occasionally he acted as an official steward of the N.A.S.C.R.C. at selected events.

The two most visual ideas that the Board came up with were purely decorative. They decided that cars were to be painted in team colours. Lea Bridge were to be painted light blue and white, Coventry were red and gold, Belle Vue had gold, red and black, Wembley had red and white, Southampton green and white and Leicester silver and black. To assist further with identification, drivers were to be allocated with their own personal numbers, which they were to prominently display on their cars. Previously these cars carried whatever number the track they were racing at had decided.

A pay structure was also agreed upon. No matter how badly a driver performed he was guaranteed £3 per meeting – even if he finished last in every race or failed to finish all of his races, he still got his £3. For all league matches team members were paid 15s (75p) a point. Payment for second-half events was slightly different, especially handicap events. Every starter in the heat was paid 10s (50p) and for the winner of the heat a £1 bonus was paid. For finishing first in the final the winner

Lea Bridge supporters club badge.

came away with £4, the second place man £3 and so on. For the driver lucky enough to go through the meeting unbeaten he could take home at least £14 10s (£14.50p), which in 1938 was a fair amount for one afternoon's work. To put it into perspective, the average wage for a pottery worker was about £3 per week.

With this rather flexible and fluid set up, the league was about to begin. The first league match took place at Coventry on Sunday 12 June, when the home side defeated Lea Bridge 44 points to 28. Just four days previous on 8 June the magazine *Speedway World* (which was not so opposed to midget car racing as *Speedway News* had been) announced that Wembley would be joining the league. Wembley had a problem though; as over 50 per cent of the straights of the speedway track was covered by Wembley's famous football pitch. Track preparation, and consequently the start of any speedway events had to wait until the cup final and any other football matches that were scheduled there were over. Furthermore, any attempt to race midget cars before the bikes was not an option; the Wembley Lion's motorcycle speedway team took precedence over all other sports held at this stadium during the summer. Once the motorcycle speedway season was underway, and the track fully prepared, then the cars could take their turn. In fact it was not until July that Wembley held their first car meeting.

As for the other tracks, the Leicester proposal had fallen through. Plans to race cars again at the magnificent one-third-of-a-mile oval at Leicester Super were well in place at the start of the season with everything fixed up for Ron Hewitt – an official with the N.A.S.C.R.C. – to promote car speedway at that track. But the then owners of the stadium disposed of the property and the new owners didn't seem to think 'Speedway racing' at their stadium was a good idea.

Southampton had run just the one meeting, this had been one of the best attended meetings to have taken place at the city's Banister Court Stadium. The stadium owners had withdrawn permission to run cars there because of the damage they perceived that the little cars might do to their beloved greyhound racing track which, like the majority of the greyhound circuits, lay outside the cinder speedway track. Nothing further was heard of Middlesbrough or Perry Bar. None of the Scottish tracks entered the league despite there being several experienced drivers from the previous season's racing at Glasgow's White City.

Edinburgh's Marine Gardens did run just one full car meeting on 2 July but never followed this up with league matches.

The league was looking very thin, as no other tracks were prepared to throw in their lot with the midget car boys. A further blow came when the news was announced that Lea Bridge was to close down! Their last car meeting took place there on 6 July, when they beat Wembley in a league match. The problem, they claimed, was that the racing was not up to standard; this was rather ironic, as this last meeting had proved to be very exciting. But the main reason was poor attendance. Lea Bridge's troubles were nothing new that year; they had earlier shut down their operations in mid-May for two weeks. They claimed that they were preparing for the start of league racing. he management hoping that enthusiasm for team racing would inject fresh impetus for their supporters. When this did not have the desired effect on attendances, a further attempt was made to lure in more spectators. By more than halving the price of admission for selected spectators it was hoped that attendances would increase. In early June the management of Lea Bridge had announced that when the supporters club membership reached 8,000 those members that were enrolled in the supporters club would only be charged 6d (2.5p) instead of 1s 3d (6.25p) entrance fee. Even though membership had not yet reached 8,000, those spectators who were already members could gain admission for 6d (2.5p) immediately, provided they helped recruit four new members to the supporters club. Even this form of 'pyramid' selling failed to bring in the necessary crowd.

All was not lost for the league competition as Ron Hewitt took a huge gamble which saved the day. He was about to open a new track. The new track he chose was Sun Street Stadium, Hanley. He felt that once the people of the Potteries had

Crystal Palace
supporters club badge.

seen midget car speedway they would be just as enthusiastic about this new sport as had the people of Manchester, when their first all-midget car speedway meeting of the season had brought in record crowds.

The infrastructure for midget car speedway at Sun Street was already in place. The stadium was neat and compact and had first opened its gates as a greyhound stadium in 1928. The following year saw a cinder track laid inside the greyhound track to accommodate the new motorcycle sport of dirt-track racing. About twenty-four meetings had taken place that year; the last one being on 5 September 1929. The track had remained dormant for motorised sport for nine years.

Stoke started their season late, eventually opening on Thursday 21 July. Stokes' team colours were silver and black. These had originally been allocated to the aborted Leicester venture. Well before the opening date publicity and preparation had been going on apace. A couple of weeks before the opening meeting the local press in the form of *The Evening Sentinel*, were carrying news of the exciting new sport. On the same day that the *Speedway World* announced the closure of Lea Bridge the Evening Sentinel published the current standings of the National Speedway Car League:

	P	W	L	D	F	A	Pts
Coventry	4	4	0	0	191	97	8
Lea Bridge	3	1	2	0	103	121	2
Belle Vue	2	0	2	0	43	100	0
Wembley	1	0	1	0	22	50	0
Stoke	0	0	0	0	0	0	0
Crystal Palace	0	0	0	0	0	0	0

As can be seen from the published league table, the name Crystal Palace had appeared. The press had pre-empted a move that was to take place between the Lea Bridge team and Crystal Palace. The Crystal Palace track had not seen midget cars for a while. The new promoter was Edward Clive, better known as 'Roy' Clive. Jim Baxter still had some control as the meetings were to be held with his assistance. This was because the whole Lea Bridge operation and team had been moved there en-bloc.

Stoke's opening fixture was to be against Lea Bridge and had been announced before Lea Bridge's move to Crystal Palace. By leaving in the two names it gave the league a bit more of a solid look, six teams were more impressive than five. The arrival of Stoke had saved the league from descending into a meaningless competition and the geographical position of Stoke balanced the league nicely.

four

Stoke's New
Team
Members

Compared to the other tracks that were in the National Car Speedway League, Stoke were late entering the fray. Coventry and Lea Bridge had been racing league matches well before the Stoke team had turned a wheel. Belle Vue and Wembley too, had driven matches. Problems with team selection and balance had been anticipated by the governing body, they devised a system of team equalisation. This body realised that the embryonic league needed nurturing during its early life.

When team equalisation was announced the well-established teams were expected to loose some of the crowds' favourite drivers. Obviously this was not going to go down too well with the supporters of the tracks that had been cheering on their favourites over the past years. Some sort of compromise was reached over this problem; it was the newer arrivals that were to be relocated. This system of relocation managed to appease some of the fans at the established tracks. Coventry kept their star driver Walter Mackereth. Similarly, Lea Bridge retained Spike Rhiando and Wembley hung onto Les White. In the north Belle Vue did much as it pleased, being fairly isolated from the more main-stream axis of the southern-based promoters. Belle Vue retained all of their Manchester-based drivers.

Leicester's misfortunes were to be Stoke's gain. In April it was expected that Leicester would be one of the League members and had been allocated several of the newer drivers who had made their debuts at Coventry during the 1937 season. Because of the failure to get the Leicester venture off the ground, the Stoke promoter jumped in and 'signed' them up to compete at Sun Street. Stoke also benefited from Southampton's decision not to run any more full car speedway meetings. A couple of drivers earmarked for the 'Saints' team found themselves 'Potters'.

For the opening meeting Stoke's star driver and captain was Cyril 'Squib' Burton; he was always referred to as 'Squib', a nickname he apparently 'inherited' from his father who was also called 'Squib'. 'Squib' hailed from Lutterworth in Leicestershire were he ran a local garage. He was no stranger to the narrow confines of the speedway tracks. Previous to taking up the midget car speedway, Squib had raced bikes on the dirt very successfully before he was forced to retire from that sport through injury. Amongst the previous teams he had ridden for was Lea Bridge. When he was competing there the team was under the promotion of Jim Baxter and his Southern Speedways Ltd consortium. After retirement, he was unable to shake off the racing bug, becoming a regular visitor to Brandon stadium to watch the midget cars there during the 1937 season. Being enthralled by car racing, he asked for a trial run, which the management agreed to, after which he made his debut in late June. After his debut the *Midland Daily Telegraph's* reporter said that he took to car speedway 'like a duck to water'. Throughout the latter part of 1937 he got better and better, and by the beginning of the 1938 season he had established himself as one of the top drivers. All the skills and track craft that he had picked up through his previous racing activities gave him a head start over other newcomers to the sport. Stoke were indeed fortunate to acquire his services.

To partner 'Squib', at number two, Stoke called on the services of local lad Joe Wildblood. Joe too had driven at Coventry the previous year. He had competed in only a few meetings, Joe had wanted to do more but pressure of business had prevented this.

Stoke captain Squib Burton.

However, for the 1938 season he had sold his business and was ready to commit himself to a full season's racing with Stoke. He showed how serious he was about his racing by ordering and taking delivery in late June, of a brand new Skirrow Special. Thus he was well prepared and ready to go for Stoke's opening meeting in July.

The diversity of backgrounds of the midget car drivers is no better illustrated than the team member who was to line up at number three. His name was 'Skid' Martin. Syd or 'Skid' as he preferred to be known, was a professional stunt driver. The pre-publicity for Stoke's opening meeting said that he had been a stand-in for several movie actors whilst filming car chases, etc. There was no doubting his ability as a stunt driver. He was to perform a couple of stunts both at Coventry and Stoke later in the season. Much was expected from this daredevil stunt and crash artiste. At the opening meeting of the 1938 season at Southampton Skid had been the stand-in reserve for the Best Pairs competition; which was the main event that evening. When he got his chance, after one of the star drivers were sidelined, he put up a terrific performance. Grasping his chance with both hands he set the fastest time of the night in heat sixteen, no mean feat so late in the programme when the track was not at its best.

For the opening meeting Skids' partner was Australian Ted Poole. Stoke had been very lucky in acquiring the services of Ted, for Ted was deemed to be the hottest property around in mid-1938. Having just stepped off the boat from Australia it seemed every track in the country was after his services. Although he had never turned a wheel in this country his reputation had preceded him. Claimed to be the Australian National Champion, Ted had raced at the very first meeting for midget cars at the Wentworth Park track about two miles from the centre of his native Sydney. On that opening night he had won two races. He later raced at Sydney Sportsground and of course at the famous Sydney Showground – which was also known as the Royal. A track that was acclaimed as the greatest and fastest speedway track it the world, for bikes and cars. It was also the track where Sir Jack Brabham was to hone his racing skills just after the Second World War. Not only was Ted a top flight midget car driver but also an accomplished all-round motoring enthusiast. In his home country Ted claimed the record for the drive from Perth to Brisbane, in the 1930s this journey was of epic proportions, considering the type of cars and the bare tracks that passed for roads in the outback. Having done the West to East route he decided to tackle the North to South route from Darwin to Adelaide, a much more dangerous adventure, where in the desert temperatures can reach 110 degrees Fahrenheit. Unfortunately, Ted's adventure ended in tragedy when his mechanic, Ken Kuhlman, who was accompanying him, succumbed to the heat. Despite this tragedy, Ted continued to pursue his motoring adventures. He arrived in England accompanied by his wife. Mrs Poole also played an active role at Sun Street, becoming a stalwart for the supporters club. Every Thursday on race night she would be seen sitting at the club kiosk signing up those spectators who wanted to join the Stoke Car Speedway Supporters Club.

The fifth member of the Stoke team was Gene Crowley, the tallest member of the team at 6ft 1in. He was always immaculately turned out with never a hair out of place, even after a hectic race; a reflection of one of his former professions as a chauffer. Amongst those he claimed to have driven for were the Duke of Windsor, then the Prince of Wales, and on several occasions he also chauffeured for the Duke of Kent. He had been driving midget cars for some time and had made his track debut in 1936 at Rye House, near Hoddesdon, Herts. This thirty-five-year-old bachelor had had quite a lot of experience performing in front of the public. He too had been a stunt driver, having performed with Putt Mossman's famous 'Speedway Circus and Rodeo Team'. One of the duties he performed in the stunt show was to drive a car as fast and steady as he could whilst Putt Mossman rode over the car on his motorcycle! This was a feat that required a steady nerve, concentration and co-ordination. The previous year he had made several appearances towards the end of the season at Lea Bridge, enjoying it so much that he was persuaded to have a full season racing in 1938.

The final member of the Stoke team on that opening night was 'Les Black'. The name Les Black was never again to appear in the Stoke line-up. In fact Les Black was a rather poor nom de plume for Les White; this came about because Stoke could only lay claim to five allocated drivers. As the venture into league racing was in its infancy, a certain amount of latitude was to be expected. The governing body didn't bother too much with strict contractual agreements between driver and club. If that had been the case an even greater farce would have developed. When drivers sustained injuries or mechanical failure intervened competitors would not have been able to fulfil team engagements. This practice of using 'guest' drivers was a pragmatic way of ensuring that teams fielded their full compliment of six drivers. As long as the system

Above: Skid Martin. (Courtesy of John Abberley and *The Sentinal*)

Right: Crash helmets were compulsory but Ted Poole prefers to pose for his photograph in the flying helmet he raced in back in his native Sydney. (Courtesy of John Abberley and *The Sentinal*)

The dapper Gene Crowley.

of 'guest' drivers was not abused too much then the paying public would put up with this system of making up team numbers. In fact the use of 'guests' is still in use in modern day motorcycle speedway, and has been in use for at least the past forty years or so. At the commencement of the league Les White was Wembley's star driver. At their first league match, away at Coventry, he scored 10 of Wembley's 22 points. So for the opening meeting, using the name 'Black' instead of 'White' somehow gave credence to the fact that all the drivers were members of the Stoke Car Speedway Team. Once the opening meeting was out of the way and the league in full swing it was expected that other aspiring drivers would come along and take part. Several venues had given trials to prospective drivers, providing them with the necessary equipment. Obviously not everyone who came along would have had the ability or determination to succeed. Track promoters openly went out of their way to recruit would-be drivers. Anyone they thought would be good enough or even someone with some sort of unusual background was coaxed into trying their hand. Belle Vue had been particularly adept at this. Amongst those that they persuaded to have a go were Jack McCarthy and George Goodly. Jack McCarthy was a Canadian whose older brother, Red McCarthy, was one of the star attractions at the ice skating show that was being put on that season at Belle Vue's Pleasure Gardens. Even if he didn't set the track alight the publicity this generated kept the crowd interested in his progress or otherwise.

The track cars that the promoters provided would have only stood up to a certain amount of punishment, so anyone who purchased a second-hand car was given a chance. It was not until later in the season that a few of last season's models were available. Harry Skirrow and his mechanics were working flat out to satisfy the demand for the latest 1938 version of his special. As the season progressed and the people of the Potteries enthused over this new sport, locals wanted to try their hand. In all, five new drivers from around the region were to put in an appearance. One of them was to go on and have a very successful motor racing career, culminating in his participation in the internationally renowned Goodwood Nine-Hour race.

five

Doodle-bug Design and Development

By the time car racing came to Sun Street the specialist racing cars that were necessary for dicing wheel to wheel around tight, loose-surfaced oval circuits were well developed. These cars had been built around the formula laid down by the governing body. As has been noted, before a workable set of rules had been set down it had been a case of 'turn up with what you've got'. Early cars had been converted specials adapted from road racing and hill climb cars. The best example of this was the chain-driven Frazer-Nash which, in 1932 in the hands of Dick Nash, held the lap record around Wembley Stadium. The same driver in the same car set up record-breaking speeds unmatched by the midget car fraternity, this time around the Crystal Palace track.

The purpose-built specials that came along were following the same route as that followed by the motorcycle speedway riders. When dirt-track racing came to England in 1928 converted road bikes were stripped down and raced around the cinder tracks. With the professional development of this sport there followed the manufacturing of specialist bikes.

By far the most successful car of this early era had been a special called 'The Gnat'. Jean Revelle built this in late 1934. This small machine with its short wheelbase of 56in, small wheels, light weight and air-cooled vee-twin J.A.P. engine was just the vehicle needed. This simple, no frills design trounced the opposition, with its enormous steering wheel and front wheel drive, it carried all before it during the 1935 season. Encouraged by the success of 'The Gnat', Revelle and two others spent the winter of 1935/36 touring Australia, where midget car racing was becoming well established, and where, fortunately, 'The Gnat' complied with the Aussie rules. The tourist put up a great show winning many friends and plaudits on the way.

It was because of the shortage of suitable cars that the manager of Belle Vue speedway had openly encouraged enthusiasts to build and bring along their creations. Not content with developing locally-built specials Mr Spence went to the USA to see for himself how the sport was run over there. He was greatly impressed with what he saw bringing back with him several Elto midget car specials. These he intended to run at Belle Vue. These small cars were a great success in the States but in this country they were to prove less successful, initially. The hard-baked clay surfaces of the US were in complete contrast to the deep black, cinder-surfaced tracks of the UK. When the Elto cars were first tried out at Belle Vue, the drivers found them like nothing they had ever experienced before! Apparently there was neither clutch nor accelerator! Their 'Evinrude Lightweight Two-stroke Out-board' (Elto) four-cylinder engine ran flat out, the only means of engine control was by the use of an advance and retard lever. All races had to be rolling starts, when the drivers were in some form of order they were flagged away.

When they first arrived, plugs were continually oiling up; the two-stroke engine wouldn't run properly at all, in fact it seemed they were a complete disaster in this country. But all was not lost. The chassis and basic layout of the car was sound.

The chassis and running gear of the Elto was based around parts cannibalised from the Model T Ford. Throughout the 1920s and 1930s in the USA every weekend at county fairs, showgrounds and trotting tracks the cars that dominated

The diminutive 'Gnat' that Jean Revelle had plans to mass produce in 1935.

One of the Elto's imported into this country by the Belle Vue management. This car is one of only a handful of cars that survive from this period.

were based mostly around the Model T. Over the years the special builder knew how to get the best out of the Model T's parts. The Elto used the front axle, chassis members and running gear, all suitably modified for midget car racing. Utilising these parts eliminated the need for expensive fabrications.

But what the Elto chassis needed was a more suitable engine. Several engines were tried including both Lancia and V8 Ford. The V8 Ford engine was too powerful for the chassis, during testing there was plenty of power and speed down the straights but drivers found themselves unable to turn left at the bends! The Lancia engine, too, was unsuccessful. The reason why this engine was tried was because one of the motor engineers who answered the call for special car builders was Len Hulme, a garage owner from Manchester, who had a Lancia dealership.

Charles (Ginger) Pashley examining the 8/80 J.A.P. engine that was fitted to the Len Hulme copies of the Elto.

Eventually Len Hulme went down the same road as 'The Gnat' and chose the V-twin J.A.P. This 1,000cc engine he mounted 'east-west' across the front of the chassis, à la Morgan Aero fashion. Unlike the Morgan, whose engine was situated in front of the bodywork, Hulme placed the engine behind the front cowl. Once Len Hulme had perfected his design, he set about manufacturing several copies of Elto chassis using the latest 8/80 J.A.P. engine.

A few other one-off specials were built and raced. Ron Wills, who had raced with varying degrees of success for the past few years, competed with his Anzani Special. A good fifteen years before Spike Rhiando built his all-alloy monocoque formula three Trimax, he had come up with his Byron Special which he called 'The Lark'. In the Manchester area, mechanic Harry Killick failed to get much further than the prototype stage. The rear engine special that Dickie Case built never lived up to the expectations we would expect today from such a layout. Some of these specials were a success, others not so. One problem was that none of the cars were built in any great numbers. Eventually, by the time car speedway reached Hanley, the special racing cars that were needed were being constructed in greater numbers and the car that was available to all was the Skirrow Special.

The Skirrow Special had been developed by Harry Skirrow. Harry is perhaps the least known and most under-rated racing car constructor in this country. It was through his drive and initiative that the most successful midget speedway cars in this country came about. He was born at Bradford in 1906 and later moved to Westmorland. He didn't start out as an engineer but as a banker. Restless with this mundane job he opened a garage on Lake Road, Ambleside. In his early twenties he had been an active member of the Westmorland & District Motor Club. During the First World War this club had become defunct. Harry was one of the prime movers behind the resurrection of this famous club. He began his racing career riding motorcycles at local Grass Track meetings. When the dirt track boom reached the North West he raced on the speedway tracks at Workington and Whitehaven. He showed so much talent, that he was on the verge of breaking into the Preston speedway team – which at that time was the most successful speedway outfit in the north of England. Unfortunately his promising motorcycle career came to an abrupt halt. It was whilst out hunting that he had a shooting accident which resulted in the loss of his left hand. This didn't deter Harry and he doggedly got on with his life. Every Saturday night, in the early thirties he was a regular visitor to Belle Vue speedway. It was here that he first saw car speedway. After watching the earlier attempts of the midget cars he decided that he could do better. Furthermore, the loss of his left hand would not hinder him from racing

Skirrow's first commercial attempt to break into the racing car scene.

cars around speedway tracks. His first car was a conservative effort compared to what he would build later. He scoured the scrap yards of Preston for the running gear of a B.S.A Scout. This he used as the basis for his first car. Back at his garage, in the space of just eight days, he constructed his first Special. His wife remembers staying up until 2 a.m. to finish painting it for its debut at Belle Vue. She said, 'It had three coats. One paint, one dust and one flies!' The car was tested at Belle Vue in 1935. Despite being the fastest four-wheel machine around the Hyde Road Circuit, Harry was not satisfied until he could equal the speed of the bikes.

The beautiful town of Ambleside was quite a distance away from oval dirt tracks. If Harry had wanted to test his car, it would have meant a huge loss of time to-ing and fro-ing. Harry even solved the problem of testing. Together with his friend, Walter Mackereth and their mechanics, they took their prototypes to the Cartmel Sands near Flookburgh, on the north-west coast of Morecambe Bay. These flat, hard sands were only about twenty miles away and were ideally suited for testing purposes. At this safe spot he experimented with various set ups. He tried rear wheel drive, front wheel drive different wheelbase and track and eventually he achieved the optimum set up. The car that came out of these testing sessions was to dominate midget car speedway.

This new car was then put through its paces on the dirt ovals. Encouraged by the car's performance and the potential this vehicle had, Harry embarked on an even more ambitious programme – he was to push the boundaries of car speedway racing even further. He was introduced to Jim Baxter at Belle Vue. Together, they were to be the prime movers behind the resurgence of midget car speedway.

He moved his family and embryonic racing car manufacturing business to London. There, in workshops rented from Victor Martin, the successful speedway bike constructor, he set about producing a Skirrow Special. On 4 August 1936, at Hackney Wick, this new car showed off its paces at a meeting grandiosely called 'The World Championship'. Here it put up a very encouraging performance. The new car was described in several of the country's top motoring and motor sport magazines. The car was both 'brilliant', 'simple', and 'years ahead of its time'. Later racing car manufacturers unknowingly used many of the features that were incorporated in the Skirrow Special. It had all-round independent suspension but the most dramatic feature was the use of four-wheel-drive. Nowadays, any car competing on loose surfaces similar to the cinders or shale of the late thirties speedway tracks needs four-wheel-drive, whether it is the ground breaking Audi Quattro through to the latest Subaru and Mitsubishi rally cars. This concept of four-wheel-drive was practically unheard of in the 1930s. The only other well known four-wheel-drive racing car being the type 53 Hill Climb Bugatti. The Bugatti's four-wheel-drive was taken through a series of prop shafts whereas the Skirrow achieved its four-wheel-drive by means of chains. The drive was taken from two sprockets on the engine's drive shafts to two 'gearboxes', one in front of the engine and one behind. From these 'gearboxes' further chains took the drive to the front and rear axles. Because of the tightness of the cockpit and for personal safety reasons, the chain that took the drive to the rear wheels was given a primitive guard; this was to protect the driver just in case a chain flew off or snapped. The driver's legs were in close proximity to the final drive, not only was there danger from moving parts but also the drivers often found their legs

The fully developed 1936/37 Skirrow special. (Courtesy of Malcolm Skirrow)

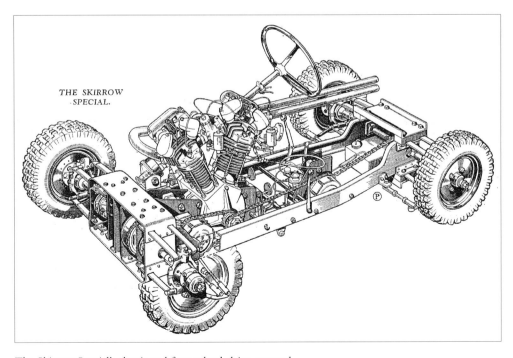

The Skirrow Special's chassis and four-wheel-drive exposed.

and shoes soaked in oil from the chains and the total loss oil system of the J.A.P. engine. The drive sprockets were secured directly to the shafts that had fabric-disc couplings, so that there was a solid drive (via the steering-head universals, of course) to each pair of wheels.

The 'gearboxes' were manufactured by Albion, as were the clutches. They were not really gearboxes as they had had all their internals removed and were in fact merely dog-clutch housings. This was because there was no need for gears around speedway tracks. There must, however, be a neutral position so that cars could then be pushed easily when lining them up for a race or when the engines were being warmed up. The lay shafts were left in place in the boxes to act as oil throws for the main shaft bearings. The dog clutches were inter-connected for operating by a lever. In addition there were two plate-type friction clutches, one on each 'gearbox' and interconnected for foot operation. As for brakes these didn't matter too much, as they were not used at all during racing. Because the J.A.P. engine ran on methanol and had a high compression ratio ranging from 11 to 1 to as much as 16 to 1 – just lifting off the throttle was enough to slow down the car considerably. In fact there was only one brake and that was on the front axle shaft and was applied by a lever outside the car's body.

A good ten years before John and Charles Cooper welded the front ends of two Fiat Topolinos to produce their Formula Three 500cc racing car, Harry had preceded this method of racing car manufacture by using the front ends of two B.S.A. Scouts. The chassis frame was contracted out to Rubery Owen and it consisted of a pair of channel-section side members expanded at the ends to accommodate the drive units. The side members were relatively close together and they were set parallel for about three-quarters of their length from the front when they tapered inwards slightly and then again ran parallel. Transverse bracing members were employed at various points, and they served to carry the cradle plates in which the engine and the two 'gearboxes' were mounted. It should also be mentioned that the chassis itself was offset towards the near side similar to Colin Chapman's Indianapolis Lotus 29. The offset was not quite as pronounced as the Lotus design. On the near-side, the four road springs had only one leaf each, whereas on the off-side there were two leaves, the extra ones being above the master leaves. The front wheels steered in the usual manner, the drive, of course, was taken through universal joints in the steering heads but at the back the wheels were set straight ahead and the track rod was bolted to the frame members so that the wheels could not be deflected. A further characteristic that seems to have been overlooked was that there were no shock absorbers on the springs!

A standard type of B.S.A. steering box was used, but it was set so that the steering column projected at an angle towards the near-side of the car. In this position it was easier to handle by the driver because the cars raced in an anti-clockwise direction; the driver, therefore, was always leaning to the left and this brought him noticeably behind the angled steering wheel. As with modern day Formula One racing cars, the steering wheel itself was quickly detachable from the top of the steering column thus enabling the driver to get in and out of the cockpit more easily. The fuel tank was mounted very low down at the rear of the car. A pump was necessary to feed the carburettor. During the early development of the car this had proved troublesome. After experimentation, a pump of

The Skirrow's off-set suspension clearly visible.

Tecalemit manufacture was fitted close to the rear gearbox where the drive shaft carried the necessary pump-operating cam. In later models – post 1937 – the tank was removed from this position and incorporated in the scuttle over the driver, and this simple gravity feed did away with the mechanical pump. It was a much more simple and efficient system and eliminated fuel feed problems. The wheelbase of the car was 6ft and the track 3ft 6in and a ground clearance was about 3in. The whole car was clothed in an attractive steel body. The complete car – chassis plus engine – cost £175. Every effort was made to make this racing car available to any aspiring driver. So, instead of having to find the whole amount, prospective purchasers could, if they wished, spread the cost by taking advantage of a flexible and generous hire purchase agreement. It was not only those who were new to midget car racing that took advantage of this concession but also some established drivers bought new cars this way. One such driver was Wembley-based Les White who paid a £40 deposit and paid off the rest of the balance with the prize money that he won from his racing.

For 1938 a whole new body shape was created. It was much more rakish and 'streamlined'. Behind the driver the tail was extended and came just above the driver's shoulder height. This not only protected the driver's head but also enhanced the appearance. The front of the car was also extended, which meant that the front wheel drive sprocket was now enclosed in the whole of the body shell. The body was slightly wider and this afforded the driver a little more room to operate. The chassis was redesigned and strengthened. One quirk with the front-

The final development of the Skirrow Special, with Harry sitting at the wheel. (Courtesy of Malcolm Skirrow)

wheel-drive B.S.A. Scout was that it was notoriously unstable at speeds above 50 to 60mph. As the Skirrow used two front-wheel-drive assemblies, tie rods were secured between the steering heads and chassis side members, which stiffened up this assembly and improved stability. The engine was moved slightly forward and this more-forward centre of gravity gave better control. For the 1938 season a problem concerning the clutch needed addressing. It was decided that, whenever possible, league and other meetings were to be clutch starts. This entailed using a starting gate from a standing start. This was a fairer method of starting races and had been used at motorcycle speedway racing for the past few years. Up until the end of 1937 rolling starts had been the norm. There had been many complaints from the paying public about drivers 'jumping' the start. The latest Skirrow had a different clutch fitted and was much more up to the job of standing starts. For those drivers who had previously purchased Skirrows they could bring their cars up to 1938 specifications for around £35.

The clever chassis design of the Skirrow would not have been so successful if it had not had the right engine. And the right engine for the job, and one that was successful right into the 1950s, was the air-cooled, V-twin, 1,000cc J.A.P. 8/80. Again, following the same course as the motorcycle speedway boys. The J.A.P. engine was to monopolise car speedway just as it dominated motorcycle speedway. The V-twin was virtually two 500cc speedway engines mounted on a common crankcase. Each cylinder had a bore and stroke of 80 x 99mm and each cylinder fed by twin monobloc Amal carburettors. The single-cylinder 500cc version was a tried and tested engine, many of the drivers of the speedway cars had previously raced bikes on the speedway tracks and knew all the idiosyncrasies of the speedway J.A.P. engine. The engine was also fairly easy to work on. Although J.A.P. had produced other V-twins, some were finding their way into Morgan three-wheelers and Brooklands Specials. It was claimed in midget car circles that Victor Martin,

Harry Skirrow and J.A.P specially designed the 8/80 for car speedway. The main difference between this V-twin and previous V-twin J.A.P. engines was that the exhaust ports both faced forwards with the inlet ports facing the rear. This meant that the top half of the 500cc speedway J.A.P., i.e. the head, barrel, pushrods, etc. just dropped on top of the common crankcase. Previous V-twin J.A.P.s would have separately manufactured heads, etc., for the rear barrel of the engine. A further problem with this design was that the rear exhaust passed rather too close to the driver. This all-new J.A.P. could, in 1938, be purchased separately for £65.

Harry Skirrow also had to persuade tyre manufacturers to produce a cover suitable for car speedway. Several major tyre firms – Goodyear, Dunlop, Avon, etc., produced the specialist tyres that the bike riders used on the dirt. But it was John Bull that Harry persuaded to produce a specialist tyre. Their previous experience in motorcycle speedway racing helped them construct the tyre that was ideally suited to the loose-surfaced speedway tracks. The same compound and tread design was copied from the bike tyres. These tyres were excellent for the job and cost 32s (£1.60) per cover, but according to an interview with Stan Mills, who drove at both Cobridge and Sun Street they only lasted for five or six meetings or no more than twenty-five racing miles. This was due to their small size of 12 x 4; the bike tyres that they copied were 22in diameter.

The right tyres needed the right wheels. It was soon realised that no matter how aesthetically pleasing wire wheels looked they were not strong enough for car speedway. Wire-spoked wheels were easily damaged. In the close wheel to wheel dicing that was part of car speedway, racing spokes could snap and wheels fly apart. Having foreseen these problems Harry designed and had made up pressed-steel four stud disc-type wheels that could stand up to the bumping and boring that took place on the track.

The fate that befell most Skirrows.

From the time Harry moved south, up until the Second World War he worked flat out producing these little cars. The only hic-up he had was in mid-1937 when he had several chassis finished and was waiting for the J.A.P. engines to be delivered. It is unknown how many Skirrow Specials were built as the Skirrow family's records of car production, together with all their personal papers and effects, were destroyed during the war when their property received a direct hit during an air raid. Some estimate that fifty were built. It was even claimed in the second edition of the book *The Complete Encyclopedia of Motorcars 1885 to the Present* – published in 1973 and edited by G.N. Georgano – that as many as 100 had been constructed. This seems rather a high estimate and a more sensible figure would be around twenty. As far as is known, two Skirrow Specials found their way to Australia. Putt Mossman, who in the winter of 1937/38 was touring that country with his Speedway Rodeo and Motor Circus, took one there. This Skirrow was later campaigned in New South Wales by Cec Garland and was one of the first racing cars to carry advertising. A second Skirrow, taken to Australasia by Bill Reynolds, could well have influenced midget car design in the United States. In late 1938 a group of American midget car drivers – amongst whom were Roy Ritcher, Swede Lindskog and Roscoe Turner – raced their rear-wheel-drive midgets against Bill Reynold's four-wheel-drive Skirrow. Later Reynolds and his Skirrow competed against two other Americans – Paul Swedberg and Beale Simmons. The unique four-wheel-drive Skirrow made a great impression on the visiting US drivers. Noting how well the Skirrow performed, the idea of four-wheel-drive was taken back to their native California; and by September 1940 Paul Swedberg was racing a four-wheel-drive car at Gilmore Stadium.

What happened to all the Skirrow Specials has not been recorded. Most of these cars would have been broken up. The car and chassis were built for one purpose and one purpose only and that was to race around speedway tracks. With neither gears nor brakes of any significance, the car was rendered useless for sprints, hill climbs and track work. Any that did survive would have had their V-twin J.A.P. engines removed as these were desperately sought after in the 1940s and 1950s. Considering the high number of cars produced – compared to other manufacturers of the thirties – more Skirrows ought to be around. At present only two complete cars are known to exist in the twenty-first century, one in this country and the other in the United States. Former classic car specialist Cheffins of Saffron Waldon sold the last known car in Britain at auction in January 2005 for £11,200.

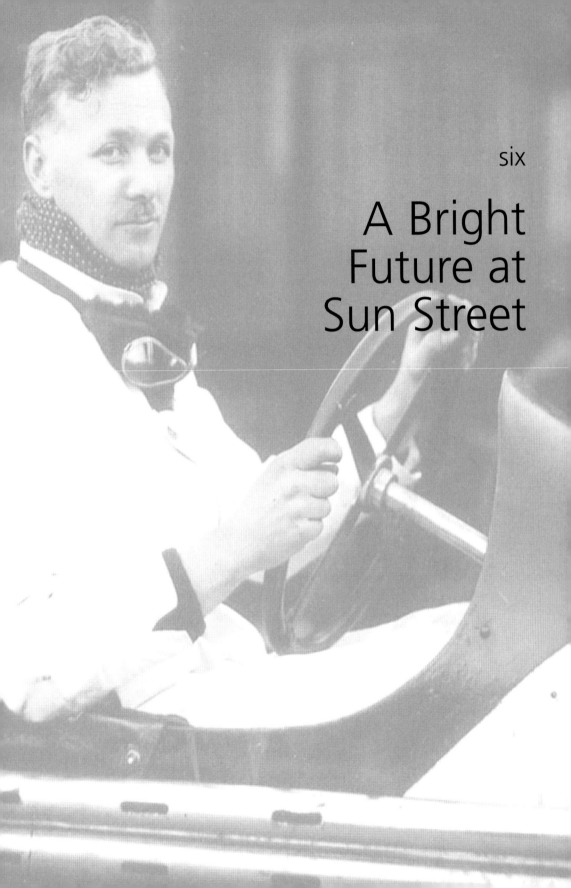

six

A Bright Future at Sun Street

At 7.45 p.m. on Thursday 21 June, four cars, two painted silver and black and two painted blue and white, dashed into the first turn of the Sun Street track; 75.6 seconds later the blue and white car of Spike Rhiando flashed passed the chequered flag, followed by the second blue and white car of Stan Mills. Spike's time was only to be bettered once more throughout the year. Stoke's start to the midget car season had got off to a dreadful start with a 5-1 victory to the visitors. The Stoke supporters had seen their drivers beaten by two very experienced contestants. Despite racing for the opposition, Spike Rhiando was to become one of Sun Street's favourite drivers – just as he was on every track that he raced at around the country, his charismatic personality winning over many admirers.

Before this first race much work had been done in getting midget car racing to the Sun Street track. The track that had been laid inside the Greyhound circuit had not been used for nine years. The last motorised event held there had been in September 1929 when Sun Street staged the sport of motorcycle speedway racing, or dirt-track racing as it was popularly known. Since then the speedway track had remained unused for motor sport. When Ronnie Hewitt took the plunge and decided to bring midget car speedway to the Potteries, he not only had to get the track in order but also had to gather around him a team of backroom officials capable of putting on a professional show. The owners of the Greyhound Stadium could supply all the necessary experienced staff to run the stadium's car parks, turnstiles, catering etc. But it was left to Hewitt to provide those knowledgeable enough and with the skills to put on an efficiently-run motor sport event. Hewitt was well capable of doing this as the previous year he had been an official of the governing body when he officiated as both a judge and steward at Coventry and Lea Bridge. As well as driving for the Stoke team, Gene Crowley and Ted Poole were involved with track maintenance. Because both drivers derived their income from racing they were fully committed to making midget car racing a success; the extra income they received from track preparation would help supplement their winnings. Gene Crowley had been persuaded by Ron Hewitt to move up to the Potteries from his native London and Ted Poole and his wife too made the Potteries their base for the duration of their stay in England. The three of them found themselves sharing the same house in Shelton. Number 9 Clive Street (now Parkhouse Street) which was only a few minutes walk away from the Sun Street Stadium. Mrs Ashcroft, their landlady, was well used to taking in lodgers at her large, commodious villa-type house.

The scrutineer, steward and judge were appointed by the N.A.S.C.R.C. Mr Hewitt took charge of the running of the meetings, appointing himself as Clerk of the Course. The important job of starter needed someone who understood all about the tensions and nervousness of the drivers before the start of a race, and Stoke were lucky enough to have such a person living locally. Although not a car driver, the person chosen to do this important job was Vic Challinor. Vic had been racing motorcycles on grass tracks for a few years and was one of the North Midlands leading exponent of this sport. A motorcycle dealer from Hanley riding his Velocette, he had carried off many cups and trophies.

Before the opening meeting publicity had been in full swing; articles and advertisements appeared in local newspapers. Similarly some of the national daily newspapers mentioned Stoke as members of the Midget Car Speedway League.

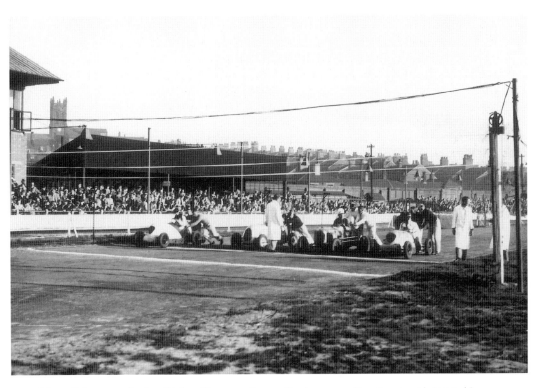

Three Skirrows and a Len Hulme Elto copy line up for the start at Sun Street, with St Mark's Church, Shelton, in the background. (Courtesy of John Abberley and *The Sentinal*)

A supporters club was set up. The success of these clubs had been demonstrated earlier in the 1930s when motorcycle speedway teams developed this form of club affiliation. This enabled supporters to feel that they too were part of the team by instilling loyalty to their team; by belonging to the club they would feel it their duty to come along week after week to cheer along their heroes. When the Empire Stadium, Wembley, opened its doors to motorcycle speedway their fully paid up supporters club membership numbered about 2,000. Within a few months this had risen to over 10,000. Many other speedway tracks did the same as it was tried and trusted method of 'brand loyalty'.

On Thursday 14 July the first advertisements inviting fans to join the supporters club appeared in all the local newspapers. The first 500 applicants would not only be entitled to the privileges afforded to new members but would also receive a 'special founders badge'. Membership entitled the supporters to all club and refreshment room privileges and amenities, supporters' outings, etc. The applicants could choose to pay either 2s 6d (12.5p) for the reserved enclosure or 1s (5p) for the popular enclosure. There were also free tickets to be won by applicants who could come up with a suitable nickname for the team; 'Stoke Lions' was given as an example but this was not to be used by the applicants. With over two-thirds of the local population involved within the ceramics industry there could only be one nickname and that was 'The Potters'.

Programme for the grand opening meeting, the Stoke management preferring to show live action rather than art work.

To keep spectators informed of the running order and who was in what race, together with short articles and gossip about midget car speedway, programmes could be purchased for 3d (1.25p). These were printed locally by T. Moston, of Cobridge. The front cover of the Stoke programme differed from those of other tracks in so much as it had a photograph of two midget cars competing against one another. The front covers of programmes from other tracks usually carried an artist's impression of what they thought a midget car looked like. If there had been any visitors to the Sun Street Stadium from Sydney, Australia, then they would have immediately recognised the front of the Stoke programme. It was exactly the same as that used by 'The Broadsider' programme from Wentworth Park, Sydney, 1935. The photograph depicted Ted Poole and Bill Thompson competing in one of the very early midget car races in Australia. As well as trying his hand at midget car speedway, Bill Thompson had competed in the Australian Grand Prix many times, winning on three occasions; 1930 and 1932 in Bugatti type 37a, and in 1933 driving a Brooklands Riley.

At this opening meeting it was reported that a crowd of 8,000 had watched this event. Whatever the number of spectators that passed through the turnstiles there were quite a number that could be added to the official figure. The whole area around the old Sun Street Stadium was surrounded by side streets full of terraced houses, a number of which over-looked the stadium and provided grandstand viewing with all the comforts of home. It was reported that some locals even risked life and limb by climbing on to the rooftops! The police were kept busy with traffic control when the stadium's official car park was full and congestion spilled over into the side streets which became packed with motors, motorcycles and cycles. All these side streets had been turned into a temporary car park. As anyone who visited the Sun Street Stadium in the 30s, 40s and 50s would know, there was a huge spoil-heap just the other side of the Clough Street entrances. This long pile of waste from local heavy industry provided a great 'birds eye view' of the stadium. This free vantage point was affectionately known by the locals as 'Scotsman's Hill'! The fame of this viewpoint was even mentioned in the following week's programme notes at Belle Vue; it was said, 'the hill was black with fans', a very appropriate description considering the colour of the spoil on the hill.

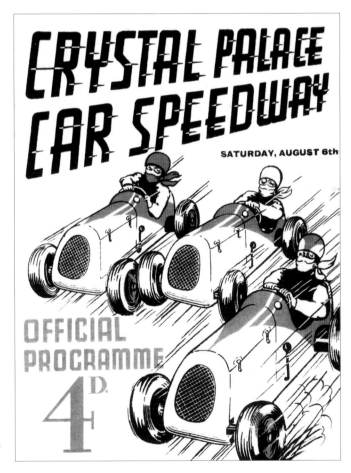

An artist's impression of midget car racing on the front cover of the Crystal Palace programme.

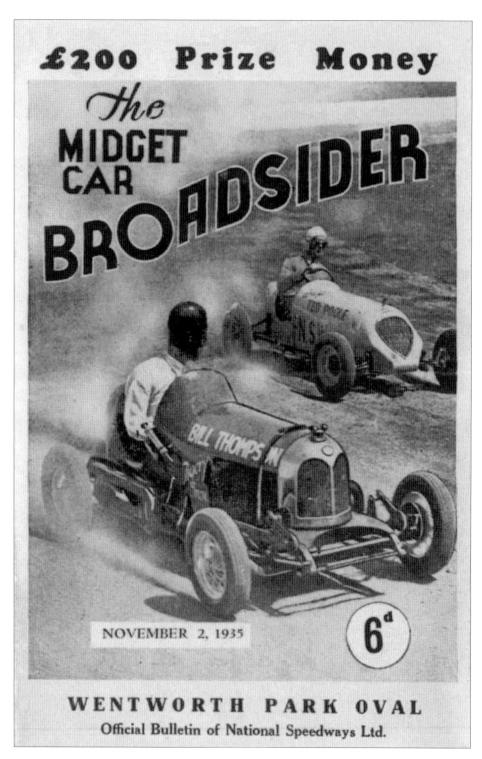

£200 Prize Money

The MIDGET CAR BROADSIDER

NOVEMBER 2, 1935

6d

WENTWORTH PARK OVAL

Official Bulletin of National Speedways Ltd.

'The Broadsider' programme from Wentworth Park, Sydney. (Courtesy of Garry Baker)

Bill Thompson and Ted Poole practising at Wentworth Park, Sydney. (Courtesy of Garry Baker)

The Stoke drivers being introduced to the public at the opening meeting; the famous 'Scotsman's Hill' in the background with its usual large group of non-paying spectators.

The second race of this opening night was also won by the blue and white of Lea Bridge. It was not until heat three that the home fans could cheer home a Stoke win. 'Les Black' led home Frank Bullock with Joe Wildblood third, giving Stoke a 4-2 heat win. It was obvious that the Stoke team was track rusty as the Lea Bridge team piled on the points and by heat eight they were leading by 29 points to Stoke's 18. But then there was a glimpse of optimism as Ted Poole showed a flash of brilliance. Living up to the reputation that had preceded him, Ted raced to a terrific win, his time of 75.8 seconds was only two tenths of a second slower than Spike Rhiando's winning time of heat one, it also equalled the time set by Basil DeMattos in heat two. Considering that the winning times set after heat two were 4 to 5 seconds slower, Ted's performance in heat nine was a terrific feat. Not only did Stoke have another heat winner but they also gained maximum heat points when Skid Martin followed him home in second place. By now the track had started to cut up badly and it was becoming very deep and rough in parts. This in some way accounted for the relatively poor performance of some of the Stoke team. With the track getting worse disaster struck in heat eleven when Ted Poole, who was leading at the time, struck one of the 'pot holes' that had appeared on the Hanley bend; this flipped him over several times. He was carried off the track on a stretcher. Fortunately to the relief of the crowd it was announced that he had sustained nothing worse than concussion and bruising. Captain Squib Burton scored a disappointing 4 points from his four races. The highest scorer for Stoke was Gene Crowley with 7 points, the rest of the Stoke scorers were Skid Martin, 5 points, Ted Poole 4 points, which included his impressive heat win, Joe Wildblood 3 points. The Potters had lost their first league match 29½ points to Lea Bridges 49½, the half point came in heat five when 'Les Black' – who scored 6½ points dead heated with Basil DeMattos for first place.

After the twelve-heat league match there were a further five races; there should have been a captains' match race between Squib Burton and Spike Rhiando, but this had to be called off because Squib's car was out of action, hence his poor score. Two Manchester drivers had been invited along; Charlie Pashley beating Frank Marsh in a special match race. The two Belle Vue drivers also competed in the second-half event that consisted of three heats and a final. The heats and final of this event were raced on a handicap system. A spectacular six car final brought down the curtain on a successful opening night's racing. This event was won by Spike Rhiando, off scratch, from Gene Crowley, 15yds, and Basil DeMattos scratch.

Although Stoke didn't win their opening league match they were determined to put up a better performance in the future. Squib Burton was particularly disappointed with his lowly score, he had been putting up excellent performances at other tracks. To rectify this Squib set about acquiring a special 'hot' motor. He sent down one of his engines to the Brooklands workshops of 'Barry' Baragwanath. He was one of the top engine experts on the V-twin J.A.P. and was the tuning wizard behind George Fernyhough's attempts on the world motorcycle land speed record attempts.

After the meeting it was obvious that the track needed sorting out. As soon as the stadium was available over thirty workmen armed with picks and shovels ripped up the bends and began to re-lay them. Gene Crowley and a very sore Ted Poole were on hand to supervise the relaying of the track. Some specialist machinery was needed to bring the track up to the standard needed for good close racing. An appeal went out for anyone who could loan them a heavy steamroller! This was needed to firm up the foundations of the track so that a dressing of red brick dust could be laid on top to form a hard racing surface. With the track re-laid much faster and better racing was anticipated and it was predicted that the track record of 75.6 seconds would be easily bettered. The Sun Street track measured 317 yards and this track record of 75.6 gave the driver an average speed of around 43mph. On the short straights it was estimated that the cars were hitting speeds of over 60mph, which demonstrated the tremendous acceleration of the V-twin 998cc J.A.P. engine.

The Speedway Car League should now have been in full swing. The 'Potters' were programmed to race their first away match at the Brandon Stadium near Coventry on the following Sunday afternoon, but all was not well with the league. As was mentioned previously, Stoke's opening meeting with Lea Bridge had gone off well. All was not as it had seemed for Lea Bridge as their track had now closed down due to lack of support. Lea Bridge had been in the vanguard of 'Doodle Bug' racing. Their track, which was around the former home of Clapton Orient football club (later Leyton Orient F.C), was one of the first tracks to open when this form of car racing was put on a sound commercial footing. Throughout 1937 they had run regular meetings; earlier in 1938 they had raced a couple of league matches against Belle Vue and Wembley. When Lea Bridge finally closed their gates to car racing their results and fixtures were taken over by Crystal Palace and this move across London allowed the league to continue without disruption. There was still plenty of time left in the season for clubs to fulfil their league commitments of racing every team twice at home and twice away – in the same way as the Scottish Premier Football League competition is run today. After this brief hiccup the league was ready to push ahead.

Stoke had a serious problem for their visit to Coventry, with only five 'contracted' drivers, the 'Potters' needed another driver to complete their squad. So instead of using 'Les Black' to make up the squad they called upon the services of Frank Bullock to fill the gap. There was, however, a more serious problem in so much as Ted Poole was still suffering from the after effects of his accident and was unable to make the trip to Coventry. When the team arrived at Coventry only four members of the team were ready to race. Frank Bullock, who should have 'guested' for the Potters, failed to compete because of mechanical troubles. Out of these misfortunes the Potters were in the long run to benefit. Les White was booked in to race in the second half of the meeting, and as usual Les turned up with his regular group of mechanics and helpers. Among his entourage was Les's younger brother, Lane. Lane had recently applied for a competition licence and was keen to emulate his brother. His chance came that Sunday when Stoke threw him in at the deep end and he took his place in the Potters line up. Although he had never raced competitively, he was more than familiar with the ins and outs of the Skirrow Special. He had taken 'The Jeep' – as Les White affectionately called his car – out on the tracks checking and testing everything. As yet Lane didn't have a car of his own so up stepped older brother Les to loan him 'The Jeep'.

MIDGET CAR RACING

AT

Brandon Speedway,

Near Coventry.

EACH SUNDAY at 3 p.m.

The Coventry promotion felt it unnecessary to embellish their advertisements.

Although this was the first appearance of the 'full' Stoke team, some of their drivers had raced there before. On 26 June a combined Wembley and Stoke team had lost 28 points to 44. Squib Burton had won a couple of races and Gene Crowley one. A fair smattering of Stoke fans had turned up to cheer on their new team. After the first race they must have been over the moon when Squib Burton and Lane White – in his first competitive race – finished first and second to give Stoke a maximum 5-1 heat win. When the meeting reached the third heat Stoke should have fielded Gene Crowley and Frank Bullock. Frank Bullock was not available and this gave the Stoke team manager a dilemma; putting out only one driver would put them at a severe disadvantage. The manager studied the rules and came up with an acceptable loophole. One of the rules governing league racing allowed for a reserve driver. The rules stated that 'Reserve drivers (if any) will be allowed to drive not more than FIVE times during the competition. If a team has NO reserve driver, any driver may act as reserve in addition to his usual place in the programme, but must not drive more than FIVE times in all during the competition'. As Stoke didn't have a nominated reserve they could use one of their other team drivers. With Frank Bullock side-lined through the legitimate excuse of mechanical problems, Lane White was sent out to partner Gene Crowley. Unfortunately for Stoke, Coventry drivers came home first and second with Lane White finishing a good third. As long as Stoke had drivers and cars ready to race they could legitimately field two drivers in every race. By heat eight the score was 27 points to 21 in favour of the home side, the Potters were putting up a good fight in their first away match. With four races to go the wheels, so to speak, fell off Stoke's gallant attempt to keep up with Coventry. A series of mechanical mishaps put paid to their challenge – this no doubt due to there being only a couple of days to prepare their cars after the hectic opening meeting at Sun

Street. Squib Burton was the Potters' top scorer with 12 points – two wins and three second places – this was despite a motor that seemed down on power. Gene Crowley scored only one point, throughout the meeting he had suffered niggling mechanical problems, a broken throttle cable, and a magneto lead coming loose and, of all things, running out of fuel in one race. In the end Stoke lost their first away match 28 points to Coventry's 44. The highlight and hope for the future was Lane White's impressive debut; considering this was his very first competitive event he scored a magnificent 7 points, which boded well for the Stoke team and gave them that extra driver they needed. The other two drivers in the team, Skid Martin and Joe Wildblood, both scored 4 points.

In the second half of the programme, after the league match, the visiting Stoke fans really had something to cheer about. The main attraction was the 'Tatlow' silver trophy. This was to be a six-car final, all the heats and final were run on a handicap basis. The three eliminating heats saw five drivers competing. The 'Tatlow' silver trophy was presented by Mr E. Tatlow, who was a keen Coventry supporter and the landlord of the Rainbow Inn, Allesley. The Coventry drivers Val Atkinson, Buster Bladon and Johnny Young had fought their way through to the final together with the Wembley drivers Bill Reynolds and Les White; the only Stoke driver was Gene Crowley. He finally sorted out his mechanical gremlins winning both his heat and the final.

Three days later, on a wet Manchester evening, 10,000 fans gathered at Belle Vue's Hyde Road stadium to see the Potters race their next away league fixture. This was Belle Vue's fifth home meeting. Their opening car meeting had taken place on 11 June when a team labelled 'The Rest' had beaten them 34-37. Having already raced four league matches, two away and two at home, they were by now 'match fit' and ready for the Stoke challenge. Two weeks previously they had beaten the powerful Coventry 'Bees', 36-33, inflicting on Coventry their first league defeat. With two defeats and a team hit by injury and mechanical problems, Stoke could only give

The *Manchester City News* populist advertisement for Stoke's first visit to Manchester's Belle Vue stadium.

their best. One good omen was that Ted Poole had declared himself fit enough to race. The big track and wide-sweeping bends of the Hyde Road circuit were similar to the tracks that Ted had raced on back in his native Sydney. A disappointment for the Potters was the non-availability of Lane White, the short notice and mid-week trek up to Manchester from his London base meant he could not take his place alongside the other team members. Squib Burton, who had installed his new motor and was anticipating a good meeting, as usual captained the Stoke team. Squib was to be partnered by Skid Martin. Gene Crowley took the number three spot. Stoke still needed to find an extra team member and they had hoped to use Jock Fergusson as a guest driver at number four, but instead they were loaned the services of Coventry's twenty-year-old sensation Johnny Young. The final two members of the team that night were Ted Poole and Joe Wildblood. Belle Vue fielded their regular side captained by Charlie (Ginger) Pashley. They were all locals from around the Manchester area and they all drove the Len Hulme copies of the Elto. The Potters started well and by heat five were leading by 19 points to 9. Squib Burton was flying and had won two races. Gene Crowley and Johnny Young too had not been headed by any of the Manchester drivers. In heat five, luck was on the side of the Potters when neither Belle Vue drivers, Frank Marsh nor George Goodley failed to finish giving the Potters a 5-0 heat win. It was also a night for accidents; in heat four Belle Vue's Acorn Dobson lost control of his car crashing into one of the lamp standards that carried the floodlighting; he was not too seriously hurt, only receiving slight cuts to his face. From heat six onwards Belle Vue clawed back Stokes' advantage; with only two heats to go they were just 4 points in arrears. Belle Vue's fight back had been assisted by the withdrawal of Ted Poole. Ted had raced to two good second places in heats three and six, but after heat six he began to feel the effects of the accident that he sustained the previous Thursday at Sun Street, he therefore wisely decided to take no further part in the meeting. With Belle Vue now breathing down the necks of Stoke, what was needed was a captain's performance from Squib Burton. Not wishing to let the side down he rose to the occasion and won heat eleven comfortably, but just as important Gene Crowley came home third. This gave the Potters a 4-2 heat win and put the match out of reach for the Manchester side. In the last race points were shared three all, Stoke had won their first Car Speedway League match 38 points, to Belle Vue's 32, gaining their first two league points.

Top scorer for the Potters was Squib Burton with 16 points; Gene Crowley had ably backed him up with 11 points. Guest driver Johnny Young scored 5 points from three drives; after suffering engine problems in his third drive he had to withdraw from the meeting. Joe Wildblood and Skid Martin scored one point each. The other 4 points came from Ted Poole with his two plucky second places, which he gained despite his severe discomfort. One anomaly of these scores was how Squib Burton was able to race in six heats, when the rules published in all of the programmes around the country clearly stated that team members were not allowed to drive in more than five races! This irregularity was due to the fact that the controlling body, the majority of whom had vested commercial interests in the sport, nominated the stewards of the meeting. This body was completely independent – they did what they thought was best for themselves; the R.A.C. and the A.C.U. having no jurisdiction whatsoever over the running of this form of motorised sport. Because there was no separate governing body who could bring to book rule-bending promoters, teams adapted the rules to suit their particular circumstances, as long as these breaches of regulations were not too blatant, the paying public were happy to go along.

Stoke's elation at winning their first league match was to be tarnished in the second half. The main feature was an event called the Irish Scratch Race, this event consisted of three heats with the winner and fastest second place going through to the final. Squib Burton had been the fastest second and had just scraped into the final. After the rolling start the four drivers hit the first bend at racing speed. Squib found himself on the outside and was trying to go around two of his fellow competitors when he clipped someone's back wheel with his front wheel. Losing control, he tore into the wooden safety fence. It took the attendants several minutes to extract him from his car and rush him to hospital. He had a badly damaged leg and cuts to his face. The X-ray revealed a severely smashed kneecap. This serious blow to Squib's promising midget car speedway career was rather ironic as he had had to retire from motorcycle speedway because of a broken leg. In fact, Squib was no stranger to injuries, in all he had been laid off through injury at least thirteen times. He had given up bikes for cars hoping they would be safer and save him from further injury.

The following evening Stoke were to race their fourth league match in eight days; this was quite a hectic start for the newly-formed team as they tried to make up for their late start. For this second home meeting the Lord Mayor of Stoke-on-Trent, Alderman G.J. Timmis, had been invited along to officially open the track. He should have performed this ceremony the previous week but a prior engagement prevented this. The visitors for this second home match were to be Wembley, captained by Ron Wills. Ron had been racing since the Twenties and was one of the pioneers of car speedway, having taken part in the very early days at Crystal Palace. At the season's opening meeting at Southampton in April Ron had been involved in a nasty accident in which he sustained a shoulder injury, this had kept him out of racing for several weeks but he was now fit and ready to take on the Potters. Backing up Ron were three other regular Wembley favourites including 'Bronco' Bill Reynolds, who at the end of the year was to make the trip Down Under to Australia. Vic Patterson and Les White were the other stalwarts of the Wembley team. Making up the rest of the team were 'guest' drivers, Wembley's official designated drivers: Syd Plevin, Vic Nield and 'Tidler' Pierson were unable to fulfil this mid-week fixture. Basil deMattos was nominated as Wembley's reserve driver, Belle Vue's Bruce Warburton and Coventry's Val Atkinson filled in for the absent Wembley drivers. Val Atkinson was in his second season of racing and had only recently been transferred from Wembley to Coventry under the team equalisation rule. Val was employed as a mechanic at the Skirrow workshops where he worked on assembling and tuning these little cars. He had a promising future in the sport and had recently won the Pendrill Trophy at Lea Bridge.

Because of the injury to Squib Burton the captaincy of the Stoke team was taken over by Gene Crowley. Skid Martin, Joe Wildblood and Ted Poole were Stoke's other 'contracted' drivers. Injury and fate still did not allow the Potters to put together a regular side. Eric Worswick from the Belle Vue team was used as one of the guest drivers and the other member of the Stoke team was Jock Furgursson who should have 'guested' the previous night at Belle Vue.

Gene Crowley being re-presented with the 'Tatlow Silver Trophy' by the Lord Mayor of Stoke-on-Trent, Alderman Timmis. (Courtesy of John Abberley and *The Sentinel*)

During the first five heats, the newly-laid track proved to be a great improvement and some of the fastest times ever recorded at Hanley car speedway were made that night. In fact in heat two Les White lowered the track record to 74.8 seconds. The meeting was one of the closest and most exciting to be held there. The reported crowd of 10,000 were on their toes all night as the scores ebbed and flowed between the two teams. Up until heat seven Wembley were ahead by 6 points. The Potters really had their backs up against the wall for in heat three they lost one of their star drivers. When making a great effort around the outside Ted Poole collided with Vic Patterson, throwing Ted's car high in the air. Unfortunately Ted was thrown out and landed rather heavily. The medical officials rushed to his assistance and after examination took the precaution of taking him to the Orthopaedic Hospital at Hartshill for further examination. It was later found that he had fractured his shoulder. Great teamwork by Skid Martin and Gene Crowley in heat eight had pulled the score back for the Potters – they were now only 2 points behind Wembley. By the end of heat ten Stoke finally got their noses in front with another maximum heat win. Once again Skid Martin was involved, this time he and Joe Wildblood edged out Val Atkinson. Wembley hit back with a 4-2 heat win in the next race. So it was all down to the last race as to who would gain the league points. The race ended in dramatic style, after four laps of wheel-to-wheel dicing and the crowd cheering on every lap, Gene Crowley and Les White crossed the line together dead-heating for first place. The 2½ points they shared for first place were enough to give the Potters their first home victory. With Ron Wills coming home in third place Wembley won the heat by 3½ points to 2½, the final score was 36½ points to 35½ in favour of Stoke.

During the interval, the Lord Mayor of Stoke-on-Trent was called upon to re-present the 'Tatlow' trophy to the hero of the moment, Stoke's acting captain Gene Crowley. The second-half individual events could have been an anti-climax after the exciting league match but an attractive programme proved to be just as thrilling. In a special three-lap rolling start match race Gene Crowley showed that his last heat win over Les White was no 'flash in the pan' when he again headed home Les in a time of 60 seconds. Vic Patterson beat Ron Wills in another match race. The penultimate race of the evening was won by Val Atkinson who led home Les White, Skid Martin and Vic Patterson. This event followed the usual second-half formula of three heats and a final, all of which were handicap races. The only driver who made it through to the final, who hadn't started off scratch, was Skid Martin. Skid had been given a fifteen-yard advantage in both heat and final. The last race of the evening was over eight laps and was won by Les White with Skid Martin second and Val Atkinson third. This race was not just a longer event but had the added twist of a 'Le Mans' style start. The cars were lined up on the inside of the track. The drivers stood by the safety fence. At the drop of a flag they ran across the track where officials – once the driver was in the car – gave a hefty push to start the cars and get them on their way. A very dangerous start procedure for those designated to push start the cars. Nevertheless, it went down very well with the spectators.

With the August Bank Holiday approaching, many locals were preparing to go on holiday for the Stoke Wakes week. The management took advantage of the holiday mood and presented an individual event called the 'Potteries Championship' on Bank Holiday Monday. For the locals that stayed at home the stadium was very busy that day, for not only was there midget car speedway in the afternoon but also greyhound racing in the morning and the evening. So popular was midget car racing becoming in the Potteries, that a greyhound had been named after the new Stoke captain, Gene Crowley. This canine racer was to be just as good as his namesake, the aforementioned greyhound winning the fifth race over 500 yards on that Bank Holiday Monday. For the Potteries Championship a field of sixteen drivers was assembled, the meeting was to be held over sixteen heats. Three Coventry drivers were entered: Val Atkinson, Frank Chiswell and, making his first appearance at Sun Street, Walter Mackereth, the finest midget car driver in England. Charlie Pashley and Eric Worswick came down from Manchester. Lea Bridge – now Crystal Palace – sent drivers Frank Bullock and Stan Mills. Local fans could cheer on home drivers Gene Crowley, Joe Wildblood and Skid Martin. The Wembley duo of Les White and Bill Reynolds made the trip up from London. Added excitement for the Stoke supporters was the debut of their new 'signing' Lane White.

Lane didn't let down his new-found fans. In his first race on the tight Sun Street circuit he finished a very creditable second behind Stoke favourite Gene Crowley. He had beaten the very experienced Stan Mills. The obvious favourite for the trophy, Walter Mackereth, failed to score in his first outing. This threw open the championship for the other drivers. Even though Walter was now out of the running he was to have an influence on the final destination of the trophy. The result of the championship was not to be decided until the penultimate heat. There were now three drivers who could lift the championship: Gene Crowley, Les White and outsider Frank Chiswell. The format for the event, sixteen drivers over sixteen heats, meant that the 'luck of the draw' played an important part in the final destination of the trophy. Usually championships were raced over twenty heats, the twenty-heat formula meant that every driver had five races and met every driver once. With sixteen heats drivers only raced four times which meant that they would not meet every competitor. As it transpired Gene Crowley never met Frank Chiswell, nor did Frank Chiswell meet Les White. The probable reason for the sixteen-heat formula, as opposed to the twenty, was to save time, thus allowing plenty of time for the second greyhound meeting that evening. The shorter programme, and therefore earlier finish, allowed some of the drivers to head north-east over the Pennines to Leeds where some of them were scheduled to race at Fullerton Park that bank holiday evening! Today, with motorway links, a bank holiday trip like this would require a certain amount of luck with traffic build-ups etc., but in 1938, with the slower roads and less reliable motor cars, it was quite an adventure. As the Potteries Championship reached its climax, heats ten and eleven were to prove decisive for Les White and Gene Crowley. In heat ten Les White came up against Walter Mackereth, in the fastest time of the afternoon. Walter Mackereth edged out Les White, inflicting the only defeat of the afternoon on Les. Heat eleven saw Gene Crowley's outside chance vanish. Gene's only previous defeat had been to Walter Mackereth in heat five. In this, his last race, he was to finish second behind Les White. Les's final total for the meeting was 11 points, three heat wins in heats three, eight and eleven and that second behind Walter Mackereth in heat ten. Gene Crowley had finished his scheduled drives and was sitting on 10 points; two race wins in heats one and nine and seconds in heats five and eleven. Heat fifteen was to be the crunch race. Frank Chiswell, almost unnoticed, had crept into a sound lead; he had defeated the less fancied runners in heats four and seven; and in the third fastest time of the afternoon won heat thirteen from Bill Reynolds and Skid Martin. In his last race Frank now faced his team mate Walter Mackereth, anything less than a win meant there would be a run off for the championship and the minor places. As it transpired Frank won the race and thus carried off the Potteries Championship Trophy with a maximum 12 points.

With the meeting over, Frank Chiswell, Stan Mills and Gene Crowley headed off to Leeds; there they were joined by Basil deMattos, Frank Marsh and Bruce Warburton. After the motorcycle speedway match between Leeds and Hackney Wick it was the turn of the cars. The first event was a series of match races: the three winners met in a final that was won by Frank Chiswell from Bruce Warburton and Gene Crowley. To add further to Frank's great day he also won his heat and final adding the Leeds Cup to his haul of successes.

Even after all the work that had been done to the Sun Street track, the racing surface was still throwing up problems. The nasty bump on the Hanley bend that had caused Ted Poole to twice have accidents and had caused several problems during the Potteries Championship needed urgent attention. The bends were again ripped up and solid concrete foundations laid in an attempt to solve the severe rutting of the bends. This method of track preparation and maintenance

The Potteries Championship Trophy which was inscribed 'Presented by Ron Hewitt won by Frank Chiswell 1 August 1938'. (Courtesy of Roy Chiswell)

Frank Chiswell winner of the Potteries Championship. (Courtesy of Roy Chiswell)

Just how badly the cars cut up the track is quite obvious in this shot of two drivers ploughing their way through the rough track.

had proved successful at Coventry, where earlier in the year similar work had been carried out on their track. The four-wheel-drive cars were notorious for chewing up the loose surfaces of speedway tracks. Where cars and bikes shared the tracks there was a certain amount of animosity from the bike riders; one car meeting caused four times the damage to the tracks. After a bike meeting it took track staff quite a while to replace and repair the surface, so one can imagine what the track surface was like after a car meeting, the base of the track would have been ripped up and great pot holes appeared. A solution to this problem was to lay down a solid foundation that would not rip up.

The track surface was not the only problem to be overcome, the next home meeting was against the top team in the country: Coventry. The Potters needed six fast and competent drivers. Regulars Gene Crowley, Skid Martin and Joe Wildblood were ready to go as was Jock Fergusson, for whom this was to be his last appearance at Sun Street. Making his home debut for the Potters was Lane White; having performed quite well – scoring 5 points (2⅓ seconds) – on his first appearance at Sun Street. Lane's racing career could only get better, so great things were expected from him. To make up the sixth member of the team the press and management announced that Jimmy deMattos was to drive. Jimmy, it was claimed, was the younger brother of Basil deMattos, the ex-Lea Bridge star. But there was a problem with this in so much as Basil didn't have a younger brother and it was in fact Basil who was driving under a false name. This not very original subterfuge was typical of the publicity stunts the promoters of the time used. They were happy to use any method to make up teams to keep the league going. A variety of drivers from different teams is more appealing to the public than the same old names and drivers appearing every week.

The visitors from Coventry sent their full team of experienced drivers: Walter Mackereth, Frank Chiswell, Johnny Young, Val Atkinson, Tony Hulme and Buster Bladon. Buster Bladon was a public health officer from Rugby and was one of the few drivers not to have a mechanical background. For the Stoke fans the great interest in John Malcolm (Buster) was that he was on his honeymoon. On the previous Tuesday he had married a local girl from nearby Crewe. His bride, Beryl Clarke, was a well-known local amateur actress. The Coventry team was on great form and they had only lost one league match, they had won all their home matches and had won away at Lea Bridge. Their only away defeat had been at Belle Vue where they only lost by 3 points. Coventry had to race the match with only five drivers because Tony Hulme failed to put in an appearance. They were also disadvantaged by the late arrival of Buster Bladon. The visitors got over this problem by replacing the missing driver with another team member in just the same way as the Potters had done on their earlier visit to Coventry when they too had a team member missing.

The work that had been done to the track paid off handsomely; the improvements resulted in some excellent racing. Halfway through the match the scores were level. Three heats later, the Potters had established a 6-point lead. However, thanks to some determined driving by Coventry youngster Johnny Young – when he finished second behind Buster Bladon in heat ten and won heat eleven – they were now only one point behind Stoke with one race to go. The odds were not in favour of the Potters as Coventry had their captain Walter Mackereth and Potteries Champion Frank Chiswell lining up against Stoke captain Gene Crowley and 'Jimmy' deMattos. The crowd was wildly enthusiastic, encouraging and cheering on the Stoke pairing; deMattos and Crowley made great starts, but, try as they might, neither Mackereth nor Chiswell were able to pass the Stoke pairing. This 5-1 heat win gave the Potters an overall win 38 points to 33 and two more league

Basil deMattos who drove once for the Potters under the pseudonym of 'Jimmy deMattos'. After the war Basil raced an F2 Cromard in several lesser Grand Prix's on the Continent.

points. Stoke's top scorer had been their captain Gene Crowley with 10 points. 'Jimmy' deMattos had three wins scoring 9 points. Lane White – on his home team debut – scored six, which included a great win in heat eight. Stoke regulars, Skid Martin and Joe Wildblood scored four and one respectively, Joe picking up his one point by finishing third in heat two. The other 8 points came from the mysterious Jock Fergusson, a name that only ever appeared three times. This name 'Jock Fergusson' drifts into midget car racing in July when he was booked to race for Stoke at Belle Vue. Within two weeks this driver again mysteriously drifts away and is never heard of again. On his first programmed appearance he was to race with the number ninety-one, but this number was later issued to Eddie Hazel who made his official debut in mid-August.

To round off an entertaining meeting there were a couple of three-lap match races; Jock Fergusson beat 'Jimmy' deMattos. Gene Crowley proved that his victory over Walter Mackereth in the team event was no fluke when he defeated him again in the captain's match race. The rest of the programme consisted of rather complicated qualifying heats and a final. This was a handicap affair, which divided the drivers into grades: the drivers returning the slowest time during the league match contested the first heat from scratch and the first and second took part in the final from the fifteen-yard mark. The other finalists were the first and second from the other two heats and they started on the scratch mark. The six-car final was won by Lane White with 'Jimmy' deMattos second, Buster Bladon third and Walter Mackereth fourth, the other two drivers who qualified for the final were Vic Patterson and Jock Fergusson.

After four successful home meetings the new sport was now established in the Potteries, a thriving supporters club was in full swing and had over 500 members, all of these members proudly sporting their black and silver club badges. One of the most hardworking members of the supporters club was Mrs Ted Poole who could be seen every Thursday evening doing her best to encourage new members to sign up. During the meetings she could be found behind a desk enrolling new members. Moreover, the sound of her Australian accent was fascinating to the locals and this great promotional asset encouraged them to spend even more time and money with her! At the supporters' kiosk, not only could supporters join the club but they could also purchase signed photographs of their favourite drivers for 3d (1.25p). These had been especially commissioned by the promoter from the Hanley photographer of 'Templeman' whose studios were nearby at 83 Broad Street. For those supporters who owned cars, or had somewhere to fly a flag from, silver and black pennants could be bought for 1s (5p).

The controlling body of the sport, the N.A.S.C.R.C., now had to make some tough decisions. From the outset they had been committed to running midget car speedway on a league basis but it was now becoming obvious to them that the league was more optimism than fact. The closure of Lea Bridge and subsequent transfer of team assets to Crystal Palace hadn't affected plans too much, but when Wembley announced that they wouldn't be honouring their home league fixtures, the whole league structure was thrown into disarray. It had been hoped that once the midget car season was under way other tracks would jump on the bandwagon but this didn't come about. The controlling body made the best of

Stoke's 1938 Supporters Club Badge.

'Flying the flag'.

the problem and pushed ahead with what they were left with. Some of the drivers from Lea Bridge/Crystal Palace and Wembley were losing out on meetings, i.e. not taking in as many race meetings as the drivers from Coventry, Belle Vue and Stoke who were now racing at least once a week. A shake up of drivers and teams was needed; the controlling bodies' team equalisation system came into play. The failure of other tracks strengthened Stoke's position. The Potters were now down to three regular drivers: Gene Crowley, Skid Martin and Joe Wildblood, possibly four if newcomer Lane White was included. With long-term injuries to Ted Poole and Squib Burton and Jock Fergusson no longer available, from somewhere drivers were needed to be found. Locals were beginning to take an interest in trying their hand at racing the midgets, but as they had neither cars nor equipment it would be several weeks before they would be competent enough to compete. At the start of the venture to bring midget car speedway to the Potteries the management announced that they were going to hold trials and provide cars and equipment to anyone who would like to try their hand. This had been done at other tracks; Lea Bridge, Coventry and Belle Vue had put on trials for would-be drivers. These tracks had an advantage over Sun Street because they didn't have to share the stadium with other enterprises that demanded track time. Belle Vue's Hyde Road Stadium was used solely for speedway racing, as long as the weather was fine the track was available; teams of workmen weren't needed to cover up greyhound tracks to prevent flying shale and cinders damaging the grass of the greyhound track. Coventry too didn't have to worry about this problem. The proposed trials for budding drivers at Sun Street never came about; the reason for this was twofold. Firstly the track was only available when greyhound racing and greyhound trials weren't taking place. Secondly, when the track was available the allotted time had been taken up by track preparation. In the early part of the season the track had been taken up and re-laid several times; the racing surface was still not bedded in enough to take the pounding that the four-wheel-drive Skirrow gave the track surface.

There had been some talk in the local press of Walter Mackereth joining the Stoke side but this was just a press release to whet the appetite of the fans. Team changes were about to take place. The Potters were to benefit from the redistribution of drivers, and two top drivers were brought in to bring the Potters up to strength. Joining the four established team members were Stan Mills, formerly of Lea Bridge/Crystal Palace, and Les White, the Wembley star.

Stan was a twenty-eight-year-old Londoner who had been born at Wembley. He was one of the pioneers of midget car speedway and had driven at Lea Bridge when that track first opened. Since then he had probably driven in more meetings than any of his fellow drivers, this was despite the broken shoulder he sustained after hitting the Lea Bridge fence during the 1937 season.

The Potters' other 'new' driver, Les White, needed no introduction to the Stoke supporters. The older brother of Stoke's promising new signing Lane, Les, had driven for Stoke in their opening meeting under the name of 'Les Black'. Fair-haired, Les had been racing since 1931, when at the age of nineteen he had made his debut at the Greenford Track. He had left school at fourteen and studied engineering at night school. He put his studies to good use by securing an engineering job at the British Salmson car company.

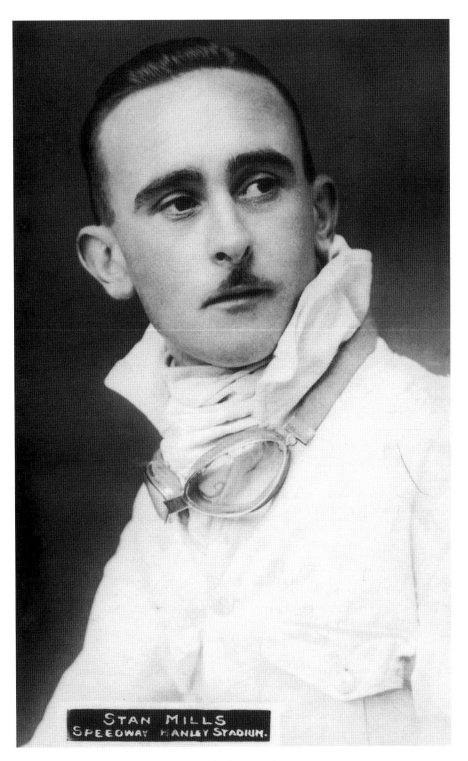

Stan Mills. (Courtesy of John Abberley and *The Sentinal*)

A less than immaculate Stan Mills with his car at Belle Vue.

With his expert engineering knowledge, he kept his Skirrow special in perfect mechanical condition. He affectionately called his car 'The Jeep'. This was nothing to do with the famous Second World War general-purpose vehicle, but was named after a character in the pre-war Popeye cartoons. 'Jeep' was a mystical dog who, when he ate orchids, was given extra strength (only in later cartoons was this idea changed to spinach). To bring him luck and 'eat up the track', Les usually raced with a white orchid fastened to the front of 'The Jeep'. Previous to acquiring a Skirrow Les had driven a very special Salmson which he had modified himself. The acquisition of Les White was a great boost to the flagging team. Les was a very smooth driver unlike younger brother Lane who was a bit wild and all over the track. He was the current holder of the four-lap rolling start record at Coventry, which was no mean feat considering the Brandon track was the 'home' of Walter Mackereth.

The track staff had worked tirelessly to sort out the Sun Street track's racing surface; the concrete foundations on the bends were a big improvement. A great meeting was expected for the next fixture on 11 August. This was Stoke's fifth home match and they were at last up to full strength. Gene Crowley captained the side at number one. He was to be partnered by Lane White. Les White and Joe Wildblood were at three and four, with Stan Mills and Skid Martin the final pairing. The visitors for this league match were the experienced Belle Vue team who were all racing their Elto-based specials built by Manchester garage owner Len Hulme. There were no surprises in the Belle Vue line up as Charlie Pashley, Bruce Warburton, Eric Worswick, Jack McCarthy, Frank Marsh and George Goodly were their usual line up. They hadn't benefited from the relocation of drivers. The way the league had been progressing, a win for Stoke would have brought them level with Coventry. But this was not to be; not that Stoke was beaten by Belle Vue, but the meeting had to be abandoned. The unpredictable English summer weather playing a dramatic role in this league fixture. The first four races went well for the Potters; they were leading 15-9. By heat five rain had started to fall. Frank Marsh won heat six; his winning time reflecting the worsening conditions. His time was nearly 6 seconds slower than heat two. With Stoke leading 21-15 the stewards had no option but to call off the rest of the night's programme. The heavens had opened up and a huge thunderstorm had flooded the track. Under normal circumstances the abandonment of a race meeting after six heats meant that the paying public were not entitled to a refund. The Stoke management decided that if the supporters hung onto their admission tickets they would be allowed in for half-price to the rearranged Belle Vue fixture. This was a very fair concession for those fans that had travelled from Manchester; they could therefore use their tickets to support their team again rather than use their re-issued tickets to travel back to Stoke for a fixture that would have been of less interest to them.

Les White sitting in the 'Jeep'. (Courtesy of Malcolm White).

Walter Mackereth added the London Midget Car Championship to his list of honours. Three days previous he had won the Belle Vue Grand Prix.

Stoke were to acquaint themselves once again with the Belle Vue team the following week, not at home on the Thursday but for their second away league match at Hyde Road on the Wednesday. When the Potters had visited Belle Vue the previous month they had pulled off their first league win, so the team had high hopes of another victory, especially now that they had strengthened the team with the inclusion of Stan Mills and Les White.

The match got off to an abysmal start for the Potters as Belle Vue raced to a maximum 5-1 heat win. Stoke's third place was gained by Gene Crowley, while his partner, Lane White, trailed well behind. This was Lane's first appearance at Belle Vue and he just seemed unable to get to grips with the wide open spaces of the Hyde Road circuit. The strengthened Potters came back and by the end of the sixth heat they had sneaked into a two point lead – Belle Vue 17, Stoke 19 – the rest of the Stoke team had been driving well. The Belle Vue team now had the services of Frank Bullock who had been drafted in after a rethink over team equalisation. He gained a second and a third place in his first two races but failed to be placed in the rest of his scheduled races. Lane White still hadn't got to grips with the Belle Vue track and in heat seven he made a great start and was leading when he got into trouble and swerved across the track whilst coming out of one of the bends. Gene Crowley, who was close behind, called upon all his experience and just managed to avoid smashing into him. At the end of the meeting Stoke had pulled off another away win. This had been a good all round performance. Captain Gene Crowley scored 8 points; Les White was only beaten once – by Frank Marsh in heat five. Skid Martin won his first three races, but he failed to score maximum points when in heat eleven he finished third behind Les White and the on-form Frank Marsh. Stan Mills scored a sound 5 points and Joe Wildblood finished the evening with four good third places, each time defeating a Belle Vue driver. Lane White did eventually score some points coming home second in heat ten.

Walter Mackereth dominated the second half of the programme. He won four races, beating Frank Chiswell in a special match race, winning his heat in the Belle Vue Handicap, and once again coming from behind to win the final, in which Les White finished third. The heats of the Belle Vue Handicap weren't without incident. In the second heat the front drive chain of Gene Crowley's car snapped which caused him to spin. Stan Mills, who was following closely, could not avoid smashing into Gene's car. Fortunately both drivers escaped with nothing more than a good shake up, and both were able to leave for home after the meeting. Although Gene had hurt his leg he was more concerned about his car; the spill had caused quite a bit of damage, the front chain had wrapped itself around the chassis and badly damaged the front end. Gene was lucky that it was the front chain, as the rear chain, which passes just below the driver, might have caused more serious damage to car and driver. This accident put Gene's chances of racing the following evening in doubt, even if he could have got hold of the spare parts he had less than twenty-four hours to get his car ready.

The last race of the evening was an event called 'The Leinster Twelve' and, in this race, a dozen cars took to the track. Les White showed all his track craft and experience to finish second behind the flying Mackereth.

The following evening, Thursday 18 August, Stoke were to stage the Tommy

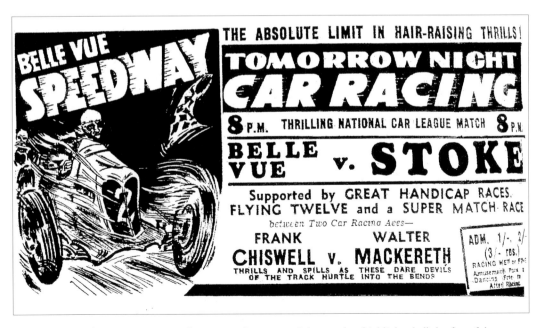

This *Manchester Evening News* advert not only promoted the cars but highlighted all the fun of the fair at the Belle Vue Pleasure Gardens.

Sulman Trophy. This was to be an individual event with sixteen drivers competing over twenty heats. Tommy Sulman was an Australian who came over to this country a few years previous and he was one of the pioneers in the sport of midget car speedway. His Singer Special won him many races before he, like all the other drivers, turned to four-wheel-drive. He now owned a small garage in London; it was here that many of the southern-based drivers took their cars along for servicing. Tommy had to retire from racing the previous year due to several accidents. After a nasty crash at Coventry he attempted a come-back at Lea Bridge in late August 1937, only for him to once again end up in hospital. It was then that a group of supporters, headed by the famous female driver Fay Taylour, asked the management if they could arrange a collection and open a relief fund for Tommy. By the end of the evening the group had collected £23 8s 9d (£23.43p). This, together with further contributions, was presented to Tommy. Having been overwhelmed by the generosity of the drivers and supporters, Tommy decided to put something back into the sport; he refused to take the money for himself and instead invested the money in buying a trophy to be competed for by his contemporaries. As recognition of his midget car racing experience he was now one of the stewards appointed by the N.A.S.C.R.C. In May grand plans had been set out and agreed for the competition.

The top twenty-two drivers were to be nominated by the controlling body and were to be split into two divisions; the first section were to race at Coventry on 29 May and the latter section were to race at another track, probably Wembley. The top eight scorers from each event were to contest the final for the trophy. Once again the organisers were over publicising their intentions; Wembley was now out of the question and other tracks were having difficulties. Original plans were abandoned and the trophy was to be competed for at Sun Street. The majority of the drivers had contested the previous 'round' at Coventry. The only exception to the original line-up was the inclusion of the four new regular Stoke drivers: Gene Crowley, Skid Martin, Joe Wildblood and Lane White. These four had replaced Squib Burton, Spike Rhiando – who were both out through injuries – Tony Hulme and Eric Worswick. At the first attempt to run the event at Coventry both Walter Mackereth and Johnny Young scored 14 points. At the time it was felt unnecessary to hold a run off for first place as the top eight were to go through to the final. Now that the original plans had been abandoned the trophy was up for grabs. The obvious favourite to lift the trophy was Walter Mackereth and his nearest rivals were Coventry team mates Frank Chiswell (winner of the Potteries Championship) and Johnny Young. Also in with a good chance was Stoke's new hero Les White. The rest of the field comprised of Stoke's other new signing, Stan Mills, together with George Turvey, Basil deMattos, Val Atkinson, Ron Wills, Vic Patterson, Jimmy Raynes and Belle Vue's Charlie Pashley. With a fast track and the top drivers trying extra hard, this was bound to be an exciting and incident-filled meeting, and those that attended were not disappointed. Halfway through the meeting Walter Mackereth, as expected, was the leading contender being unbeaten. The majority of the drivers had dropped points to one another; Les White, had been beaten twice, once by Mackereth and once by Ron Wills. Both Frank Chiswell and Johnny Young had ruined their chances by finishing third in their respective heats. The surprise of the night had been Lane White who had won both his opening races, and he was about to face Walter Mackereth in heat eleven. This was to be the vital race; Lane White made a good start and was out in front, by the second lap Mackereth was right on his tail and made a tremendous effort around the outside. Wrestling with his car he got into the deep rough surface that had been thrown up near the perimeter of the track; Walter hit the fence, but somehow he quickly got his car under control and set off after the other three drivers. With the crowd roaring their approval, he passed one driver and on the last bend caught up with Val Atkinson and the pair of them crossed the finish line together. The steward of the meeting could not separate them and declared a dead heat for second place, both being awarded 1½ points each. Lane White had won the race in the fifth fastest time of the evening putting him into a great position to win the trophy. In the heat previous to the Mackereth incident, Skid Martin and Jimmy Raynes had collided with one another; fortunately neither of them sustained any damage to themselves or their cars. In heat fourteen there were only two finishers; Frank Chiswell leading home Les White. The other two drivers, Johnny Young and Basil deMattos, had a coming together, as a result of which Johnny Young's car overturned. Fortunately Johnny was only shaken. Walter Mackereth was involved in a further incident in heat seventeen when he came into contact with the unfortunate Skid Martin. Charlie Pashley and Basil deMattos, who were close behind, had nowhere to go and consequently all four cars piled into one another. Damage to car and drivers could have been much worse had it not been for the quick reactions of Basil deMattos, as he skilfully slid his car sideways to lessen the force of the impact. Skid Martin's car was far too badly damaged to take part in the re-run of the race; which was won quite easily by Mackereth. This was Walter's last scheduled drive and he finished the meeting with 13½ points. It was now up to Lane White, the pressure was on him, he had to finish first or second. He need not have worried as, making his usual lightning start, he overcame Gene Crowley and Jimmy Raynes, to give him a fifteen point maximum to win the trophy. In his short career this was his best result, a magnificent performance for someone who only started his competitive career the previous month. Walter Mackereth's 13½ points put him in second place. Frank Chiswell recovered well winning his last two races and finished third with 12 points.

At the start of the meeting Gene Crowley had been a doubtful starter, having badly damaged his car the night before at Belle Vue. His inclusion in the meeting had been down to the charitable generosity of local garage owner Cecil Heath of Cobridge. Although the track had been unavailable for trials this hadn't prevented certain locals who were determined and enthusiastic enough to want to try out this form of motor racing. Two such locals were Reg Grice and Cecil Heath as both had decided to purchase Skirrow specials. On the afternoon of the Tommy Sulman Trophy Cecil Heath had taken delivery of a Skirrow Special. This had been brought to the Sun Street track by Walter Mackereth, who was the manager at the Skirrow workshops. Walter gave the car a shakedown around the track before Cecil took his first tentative laps around the track. The general opinion of those present that afternoon was that Cecil had the makings of a competent driver. It was this car that Cecil had just taken delivery of that Gene Crowley used that evening. The Stoke captain's low score of 6 points, from a win, 1⅓ seconds, probably accounted for by his reluctance to push his loaned car too far. At the back of his mind was the fact that he had to keep the car in one piece for a special match race that Reg Grice and Cecil Heath were to have after the main event. The match race duly took place and was easily won by Reg Grice.

Reg was from Stafford and the car that he had recently purchased was one of the fastest and well-sorted midgets around. The car he had acquired had formerly belonged to Squib Burton. The accident that Squib had sustained at Belle Vue was to finish his racing career. The knee injury, plus all the injuries Squib had sustained during his motorcycle speedway career, convinced him that it was time for him to give up competitive motor sport, reluctantly selling off all his racing equipment.

The following week it was back to league racing, with the Potters taking on Belle Vue. Once again Stoke fielded their strongest team: Gene Crowley (captain), Lane White, Les White, Joe Wildblood, Skid Martin and Stan Mills. The Belle Vue team regulars still remained faithful to their rear-wheel-drive, Len Hulme copies of the Eltos. Away from the wide bends and long straights of Hyde Road the Elto's were becoming uncompetitive, and, consequently, Len Hulme was discussing the idea of a new drive configuration for his cars. Not all the Belle Vue team was aboard Eltos, as Bill Reynolds and Vic Patterson were using Skirrows. These two drivers had been drafted into the Belle Vue side to give the Manchester team a bit more strength away from home. They had been 'transferred' north when their home track of Wembley had dropped out of the league. The match was very one-sided, mainly due to mechanical problems with the Belle Vue cars. Stoke easily won 49 points to 29, this was despite the fact that the Potters captain, Gene Crowley, failed to score any points. Gene was still having problems from the previous week's smash at Belle Vue. Only Bill Reynolds, with 9 points put up any opposition to the Potters. Neither Les White nor Lane White were beaten by an opposing driver. Lane registered four wins to give him a twelve point maximum, Les scored 13 points from five drives for the rest of the Potters; Skid Martin scored eleven, again from five starts. Both Skid and Les had extra starts as replacements for the off-form Gene Crowley. Stan Mills managed 5 points and Joe Wildblood, having one of his best meetings so far, scored 8 points. The thirteen other points that Belle Vue scored came from Frank Marsh with six, Eric Worswick five, George Goodly and Vic Patterson one each.

The second half of the programme saw Lane White enhance his reputation even further when he won his second trophy in successive weeks by winning the handicap event. For winning this event Lane was presented with the Hanley Cup by Miss Mary Bell who was the current North Staffs Royal Infirmary Queen. The White family was now on the crest of a wave, and the brother's proud father felt that his two sons were the best drivers around. Walter Mackereth had other ideas, a certain friendly rivalry had developed between them, and this went back several weeks. It was during the Potteries Championship, that Mackereth's win over Les White had prevented Les from winning the championship; conversely Lane White's win over Walter, in the Tommy Sulman Trophy had dented Walter's chances of him taking that trophy. Now that Lane was going so well his father believed that Lane was now the fastest driver on the circuits and was prepared to-back this up monetarily. Mackereth was prepared to accept any challenge and Lane's father put down £20 for a special match race; Walter responded with his

Crystal Palace's advert for the Fourth Test Match.

£20, so a series of special match races was set up. The winner of the best of three races would walk away with the £40! The arranged date for this wager was to be Stoke's next home meeting on 1 September when the Potters were to race a league match against Crystal Palace.

Two days later, at Crystal Palace, the White brothers were in action again, not in a league match or individual event, but driving for the South of England in the fourth 'Test Match' of the North v South series. The joint efforts of the White brothers gave the South their first victory in the series, winning 65 points to the North's 43. Les, the captain of the South, was their top scorer with 14 points, but it was Lane who once again stole the limelight with a very creditable thirteen. Walter Mackereth, who captained the North, went through the meeting unbeaten to score 18 points from his six drives. These defeats for the White family added more edge to the forthcoming match race.

The eagerly awaited match race ended in disappointment, for the next day, on the Sunday at the Rye House track near Hoddesdon, Hertfordshire Lane, White crashed heavily. Lane had been participating in a stunt show that was touring Great Britain at the time. Apart from the usual trick riding and comedy routines, motorcycle speedway racing and midget car racing made up part of the bill. Although the circus and rodeo had its own full time personal, other semi-professional drivers and riders were invited along to test their skills against the highly accomplished stunt artists who made a living from their motor-robics. It was whilst giving a demonstration of midget car racing that Lane sustained a fracture to his left arm and this was to put him out of action for several weeks. Not being perturbed too much by his younger brother's accident, Les said he would step into his shoes and take up the challenge that Walter Mackereth had accepted.

The loss of Lane White posed the problem of who would be his replacement for the next home league match, which was to be against Crystal Palace. One good piece of news was that Ted Poole's shoulder was now out of plaster and he was eager to get back onto the race track. First he needed to get fit, as he was still stiff he felt he was not yet ready to make his comeback. The previous week a match

Lane White was featured on the bill with the Putt Mossman stunt show.

race had taken place between Joe Wildblood and Reg Grice. Although Joe won the race Reg had done enough to convince the management that he was worth a try in the Stoke team.

To gain more experience, Reg had been included in the line up for the Pallatine Trophy at Belle Vue. This had taken place on the night before the Crystal Palace match. Other Stoke drivers who competed in the event were Les White and Stan Mills. The event was won by Walter Mackereth, whose time in the opening race had broken the track record for cars, his time of 76.6 seconds was only 0.6 of a second slower than the bike track record held by Frank Varey. This winning time was to remain unbeaten and was still published in the Belle Vue programmes list of track record holders right into the late 1940s. But Walter did not have things all his own way that evening, as in the heat of the 'Treble Six' event, he was beaten by Les White.

The line-up for the Crystal Palace match was: Gene Crowley (captain), Reg Grice, Les White, Joe Wildblood and the useful partnership of Stan Mills and Skid Martin.

The Potters now had sufficient drivers on their 'books' and were able to nominate a reserve driver. Newchapel-born Cecil Heath was given the role as Stoke's number seven. The Crystal Palace team was packed with fast, experienced drivers. They were captained by Spike Rhiando, who was partnered by Eddie Hazel. George Turvey, Frank Bullock, Jimmy Raynes, and Basil deMattos made up the rest of the team. Unfortunately the night before at Belle Vue, Basil deMattos had been involved in a nasty accident where he received head injuries and bruises, so he was out of midget car racing for a while. A 'guest' driver took Basil's place in the team. This was former Wembley star Bill Reynolds. The Potters had been hoping to avenge the heavy defeat that they had suffered at the hands of the Crystal Palace drivers on the opening night of the Stoke season when they lost to the then Lea Bridge side. The Potters' supporters were now more optimistic of gaining revenge for their defeat now that they were fielding a more experienced team. After just two races Stoke found themselves 6 points behind; by heat six, the half-way mark, the deficit had been reduced to 4 points. Over the next few heats Stoke were unable to pull back any further points and going into the last heat they were still 4 points behind. The Potters now had no chance of winning the match and the most they could hope for was a draw. Les White and Gene Crowley faced Spike Rhiando and Bill Reynolds. Les White had been beaten twice by Crystal Palace's George Turvey; Gene Crowley had only managed three third places. The biggest crowd of the season saw White and Crowley make good starts and shoot to the front. With the two Stoke drivers in the lead and blocking every move made by the Crystal Palace drivers, the Potters drivers finished first and second. This 5–1 heat win was enough for the Stoke team to snatch a draw. The heat win gave Les White 10 points and Gene Crowley's second place meant he finished the evening with 5 points, but he was still struggling to find the good form that he had shown earlier in the season. Stan Mills had three heat wins and a third to give him 10 points, Skid Martin, a solid seven, Joe Wildblood managed three and Reg Grice, on his debut, scored only one point by finishing third in heat ten. In the league match Crystal Palace had only used five drivers. Jimmy Rains had failed to turn up. His place, on each occasion, was taken by the other Crystal Palace drivers, which was allowed under the loosely-worded rules. George Turvey was Crystal Palace's top scorer with 13 points followed by Eddie Hazel with ten, Frank Bullock with five and a subdued Spike Rhiando with five; Bill Reynolds scored 3 points.

Although Reg Grice had only scored one point, the experience of racing wheel-to-wheel with the top drivers was to be of benefit later that night. The main second-half event was handicap-based. Reg won both his heat and the final. Not wishing to take anything away from Reg's performance it did highlight the fact of how difficult it was to pass on the Sun Street track. Because of his inexperience he had been given fifteen yards start on the likes of Stan Mills and George Turvey, both of whom had scored well in the team event and yet were unable to get by Reg.

As for Stoke's other debutante, Cecil Heath, he was not called upon to race in the league match. In the Inverted Handicap event he finished third behind Skid Martin, who was off scratch, and Joe Wildblood, who was also given fifteen yards start, the same as Cecil.

The much-anticipated match race between Les White and Walter Mackereth was settled in just two races. In the first race those present witnessed the rarity of

Walter Mackereth being sidelined by engine failure. For Walter this was indeed usual as he had the finest and best prepared equipment in the sport. He was virtually the 'works' driver for Skirrows. The second race saw Les White take the £40 stake money when he won the race in the fastest time of the night, albeit from a rolling start.

The next meeting to be staged at Sun Street was the biggest team event of the year; this event was to be held over eighteen heats as opposed to the usual twelve. This star event was the final and fifth official Test Match between the North of England and the South of England. The event was billed as the deciding match in the series. All the local advertising in the previous week's programmes and in the local press, stated that the South had won at Coventry and Crystal Palace, and the North had taken the honours at Belle Vue and Leeds. Therefore the series was delicately balanced. All the pre-race publicity was centred on this being the decider. If in 1938 there had been an Advertising Standards Authority then Provincial Car Speedway Limited, the promoters of midget car speedway at Sun Street, would have been in serious trouble! The North, on 3 August, had won 60-47 at Belle Vue, and again at Leeds 54-53 on 22 August, the North also won 59-49 at Coventry on 10 July, which was the first match in the series. To give the meeting extra appeal mendacious advertising had blatantly misled the public. With the Stoke season opening after the Coventry event it was doubtful if any of the regular paying public knew the results of the previous encounters, the only knowledge they would have had came through programme notes and what the promoters had told the local press. There was little or no coverage in the national press nor was there any publication devoted solely to midget car speedway.

The governing body had decided to select the teams on the premise of where the drivers were born and not for which team they drove for nor where they now lived. This saw several team mates on opposing sides; Stoke fans saw Les White, Gene Crowley and Skid Martin line up for the South. Loyalty of the Stoke fans was put to the test. Did they cheer for their drivers representing the South, or for the northern team? Stoke was more northern than southern, but the northern team contained Coventry drivers Walter Mackereth, Johnny Young, Val Atkinson and Buster Bladon who were all the Potters most deadly rivals. The other two drivers for the North were Belle Vue's Eric Worswick and Stoke's Stan Mills; the nominated reserve was Joe Wildblood. Apart from the Stoke drivers, the South's team was made up of George Turvey, Frank Bullock and Frank Chiswell. Apart from hoodwinking the public into thinking that this Fifth Test was the decider, there was one further misnomer. Stoke's Gene Crowley had driven for the North in the Fourth Test at Crystal Palace, scoring 2 points.

The score throughout the meeting was very close and after fifteen heats the score was level at 45 points all. From a promoter's point of view, if the pre-race publicity was to be believed, this was an ideal situation, with three heats to go there was still nothing in it. The whole series apparently now depended on the last few races. There were a few problems to overcome before these heats took place. Les White, the South's captain, was unable to take his last drive, as in heat thirteen he suffered from mechanical gremlins. In his previous races he had won three and finished second in his other drive. Gene Crowley still had not regained form and had been replaced in his previous drive; in fact he competed in only four of his six

The only Belle Vue driver in the North's team, Eric Worswick is shown here wearing his distinctive striped cravat.

scheduled drives. As for the North, Stan Mills had had to pull out of the meeting after his first race, in which he had finished third. Once again there were some liberal interpretations of the rules, the paying public didn't seem too concerned about the niceties of the rules. When a driver was unable to take his scheduled drive he was replaced by one of his team mates; so it was that Johnny Young drove in eight races, two more than his programmed six. He had taken the place of Stan Mills twice, once in heat twelve and again in heat sixteen. Similarly, Walter Mackereth stepped into the slots vacated by Eric Worswick in heat sixteen and Val Atkinson in heat eighteen. Most of these substitutions came about because of the temperamental Skirrow Special. Despite the usual reliability of the J.A.P. engine, it was the clutch starts that were taking the toll on the cars. The extra drives that Mackereth took meant that he drove in the last four races, all of which he won! In two of these races, heats sixteen and the final heat eighteen, he had been paired with Johnny Young, it was this pairing that ensured victory for the North. In the last three races the North won the heats 5-1, 4-2 and 5-1 respectively, to give them victory with 59 points to the South's forty-nine. This meant that the Stoke fans believed that the North had won the series three–two, but in actual fact it had been a four–one victory. With their extra drives, Mackereth and Young had scored over two-thirds of the North's points, Young scored 22 points and Mackereth eighteen. The other 19 points came from Buster Bladon with eight, Eric Worswick with two, Stan Mills with one and from the reserve slot Joe Wildblood managed 6 points. The South's top scorer was Potteries champion Frank Chiswell with thirteen, Les White and George Turvey both scored eleven, Frank Bullock eight and Stoke's Skid Martin four. As for Gene Crowley, he only managed 2 points from four drives. Gene Crowley's depressing run was further compounded when it was announced later in the press that he was to relinquish the captaincy of the Potters and hand it over to Les White. To complete the night's entertainment two match races were added to the programme. In the first, the top scorers from each side met over four laps rolling start. This saw Frank Chiswell beat Johnny Young. The second match should have been between the two reserves – as the South's reserve Eddie Hazel was unavailable, the scheduled match race was replaced by the evening's two captains. Once again, Les White and Walter Mackereth resumed their on-track rivalry. This race was again over three laps with a rolling start. Les White proved that the previous week's victory over Mackereth was no fluke. He won the match race and lowered the three-lap rolling start track record to 58.6 seconds.

It was a return to league racing for the next home meeting when Coventry were due to visit Sun Street for their second league match. There were no major changes to the Stoke side except that Les White now captained The Potters. The added pressures of the captaincy had perhaps compounded Gene Crowley's lacklustre performances since his car was badly damaged a few weeks earlier at Belle Vue. With this pressure removed and the assistance given to him by Stoke's promoter, Mr Ronnie Hewitt, in the form of a brand new Skirrow Special, better things were now expected from Gene. Coventry were tough opposition, having only lost two league matches all season. True to form, they were all set for another league victory as by heat eight they were 8 points ahead and there were only four heats to go. The gap between the more experienced Coventry drivers and Stoke's newcomer Reg Grice was really beginning to show. Reg had finished last in his first three drives. Heat nine saw the Potters stem Coventry's advance towards victory when Gene Crowley and Joe Wildblood started to turn the tide with a four–two heat win. In the next race, heat ten, the Potters sent out Les White, in place of Reg Grice, and Stan Mills, in place of Skid Martin. These easy going adaptations of the rules benefited the Potters when the pair defeated Ron Wills and Buster Bladon, to put them within 2 points of Coventry. Stan Mills was out again in the next race but mechanical failure halted the fight back when Stan went out with car trouble, leaving Joe Wildblood to lead home Johnny Young and Val Atkinson. It was now all down to the last heat. Les White and Gene Crowley were to face Walter Mackereth and Frank Chiswell. To win the match White and Crowley had to finish first and second, a tough assignment against the high-flying Coventry pair. Fortune smiled on the Potters because Walter Mackereth had clutch trouble at the start and was compelled to retire. The Stoke pair raced into the lead, Les White winning from Gene Crowley and Frank Chiswell in the second fastest time of the night, only Mackereth in heat one bettered his time. A

One of the *Evening Sentinel* adverts keeping supporters abreast of events. (Courtesy of the *Sentinel*)

feature of Stoke's 37-35 victory had been the return to form of ex-captain Gene Crowley, who scored a much-improved 10 points, the new car performing and handling well. The new car brought to Gene the confidence in his equipment that had been lacking since the Belle Vue incident. Stoke's other two star drivers, Les White and Stan Mills did well also. Les scored 12 points and Stan 8 points. Stoke's other 7 points came from Joe Wildblood, with four, and Skid Martin, with three. Unfortunately for Reg Grice he failed to score. The Coventry team put in a much more solid all-round performance. Their lowest scorer was Ron Wills with three and their highest Walter Mackereth with eight. Between these two, Val Atkinson and Frank Chiswell both scored seven; Johnny Young and Buster Bladon scored five each.

The second half was composed of a series of match races and the now familiar handicap event with a six-car final. In the first heat of the handicap event neither of the two new local drivers, Reg Grice and Cecil Heath, advanced to the final, despite both being given fifteen yards start. The first event was won by Basil deMattos. Often drivers from other tracks would be invited to appear in second-half events, competing in special match races, two, three or four-lap record attempts or in the main feature events – either handicaps or scratch. So it was that Basil deMattos made the trip up from London, he was to have three drives in the second half. He competed in a match race against Skid Martin, won his way to the final by winning heat two of the handicap event and finally won the six-car main event from Val Atkinson and Stan Mills.

This had been Stoke's tenth meeting of the season and the supporters club was flourishing. In two weeks time, on 30 September, the supporters club was to hold a speedway supporters club ball at the Grand Hotel, Hanley, which, as the name suggests, was the largest and best hotel in the Potteries. All sorts of novelties had been arranged for the evening and the locally renowned Dave Price and his band had been engaged for the evening. Tickets for the ball were on sale at 3s (15p) with dress optional. This end of the season bash had been granted an extension to the licensing hours with the fun continuing through until 2 a.m. Many of the drivers had been requested to attend and were expected to make the trip to Stoke. One of the advantages of being a member of the supporters club was that they had access to the Club-House. This, in actual fact, was the main bar area and was situated above the main grandstand on the start and finish straight. As membership grew this faculty became more and more crowded and, eventually, complaints were made to the management that non-members and the general public were being allowed into this area. Admission to this part of the stadium was only allowed if members were wearing their allotted member's badge. The management, wishing to keep faith with their supporters, followed up these complaints and found that a good majority of those using this facility were members of Hanley Greyhound Club, and they too were entitled to use the stadium's facilities. Thus, the appeal of midget car speedway reached out beyond the car enthusiast.

Interest in this new sport had spread and for those who were curious enough and who didn't have a car nor wished to drive to Hanley could come along to Sun Street by specially laid-on public transport. The LMS railway advertised a special train service from the south of the county. Starting at Hednesford (now the home of the Midlands most famous short circuit oval) the train stopped at Cannock, Wryly, Walsall, Darlaston, Willenhall, Wolverhampton, Stafford and finally Stone before reaching Stoke station where special buses would take passengers to nearby Sun Street. Providing there was no delay, supporters would arrive with plenty of time to spare. Similarly, the return journey coincided with the end of the meeting.

For those supporters who wished to cheer on the Potters at their next away league match at Coventry, a bus trip was arranged by the supporters club. The cost of the trip was to be 4s 6d (22.5p), but this didn't include admission to the stadium. As a special dispensation to the visiting Stoke fans, the Coventry management arranged for them to be charged 1s (5p), which allowed them to spectate from any part of the stadium. The buses were to leave the Sun Street car park on Sunday at 11 a.m. prompt and the return journey was to commence at 6.30 p.m. Food was not provided and fans were encouraged to bring along picnic lunches. Tickets for the trip were available from the supporters' club outlets near the Popular and Reserved clubrooms. In charge of these arrangements was Mrs Ted Poole, who was still helping out with the organisation of the club as well as helping with the convalescence of her husband, who was desperately hoping to get back to racing. With plenty of vocal support the Potters were hoping to end Coventry's domination of the league. Having beaten Stoke earlier in the year and having never been beaten at home, Coventry fans were confident they would pull off another victory. Coventry's local newspaper, the *Midland Daily Telegraph*, was not so sure, and they described the Potters as 'formidable opponents'.

Coventry supporters club badge. (Courtesy of Ian Sommerville)

Stoke sent the same team that had just beaten Coventry at Sun Street, three days previously. Coventry, too, fielded the same side. By the end of heat seven, Stoke were only one point behind the 'Bees', Coventry leading 21 points to 20. An encouraging feature of the match so far had been the determined driving of Stoke's two newcomers. Although he had failed to score in his first race at the Brandon circuit, Reg Grice had followed home Les White in heat four, beating Buster Bladon and Johnny Young, who unfortunately had suffered mechanical troubles. Again, in heat seven Grice followed home White, this time, however, the points were shared three all as Frank Chiswell raced ahead. In heat five Joe Wildblood was unable to take part and Stoke sent out their reserve, Cecil Heath. This was the first time that Cecil had raced for the team and he wasn't overawed by the occasion and finished a great third to claim his first point for the team. The large number of Stoke fans who had made the journey shouted, clapped and cheered every effort made by their team. By the end of heat ten, thanks to a 5-1 win in heat eight by Walter Mackereth and Ron Wills, Coventry had slipped into a 32-27 lead. Heats nine and ten had seen the points shared. Reg Grice's second place in heat ten was particularly encouraging. This boded well for the future as he seemed to improve with every outing, his performance on the Brandon track was much better than three days before at Sun Street when he had failed to score a point. The faster and more sweeping bends of Coventry were much more to his liking. With only two races to go and five points in it, the travelling Stoke supporters were hoping their team could come from behind and pull off another late win. The penultimate heat saw Gene Crowley and Skid Martin face Frank Chiswell and Buster Bladon. This time there was no dramatic last heat decider as Frank Chiswell won from the Stoke pairing. The last heat was an anti-climax unless both Coventry drivers failed to finish! With Walter Mackereth and Johnny Young this was highly unlikely; but Les White did manage to split the Coventry pair. Coventry's last league match ended in victory for them 39-32. The Potters had driven well and their performance, encouraged by their vocal supporters, was even more outstanding when one takes into account the mechanical problems the team had encountered. Gene Crowley's car never arrived, Joe Wildblood and Les White had 'blown' their motors, Stan Mills too had motor trouble. Fortunately for Stoke they had taken along to Brandon their spare track car; it was this car that Gene Crowley had used throughout the meeting. When other Stoke drivers had problems they too jumped into the spare car. Apart from a few moments between heats, this car was raced nearly all afternoon. Les White was Stoke's top scorer with eleven points from five starts, Gene Crowley continued his return to form with seven, Skid Martin scored six and the surprise of the afternoon Reg Grice with a well-driven five points. Joe Wildblood, and an off-form Stan Mills only had one point each, as did Stoke's debutante at reserve Cecil Heath.

Frank Chiswell and Walter Mackereth had both gone through the meeting unbeaten. Mackereth unfortunately had mechanical trouble in his second drive and scored nine, as did Ron Wills – who had been loaned to Coventry from Wembley earlier in the season. Johnny Young scored seven, Buster Bladon two and an unfortunate Val Atkinson failed to score as he was dogged by mechanical trouble all afternoon, an embarrassing situation for him as he was a member of staff at the Skirrow Workshops.

It had not been a particularly good day weather-wise. There had been some rain in the afternoon. The greasy track caused one or two scary moments, the track conditions playing into the hands of those drivers who managed to get to the front quickly; this was illustrated no more so than in the second-half handicap event. Before the heats and final of the 'inverted' handicap, the two fastest drivers from each team met in a three-lap rolling start match race; this was won by Les White who defeated Johnny Young. The handicap event featured two heats with six drivers in each heat, the first three going through to the final. In the first heat, Reg Grice won from Ron Wills, both drivers having been given fifteen-yard starts. Third had been Johnny Young from scratch. The second heat showed what a great track master Walter Mackereth was when, despite the deep and greasy track, he came from the back to beat Buster Bladon – off fifteen yards – and Les White, who too had done well to come through the field to finish third. The same handicaps were used in the final. Reg Grice got the drop on the other two drivers off fifteen yards and took the lead. Walter Mackereth fought his way up to second and on the

HANLEY SPEEDWAY

TO-MORROW (Thurs.)

CHALLENGE MATCH

STOKE

v.

CRYSTAL PALACE

The only team to win
at Hanley.

SKID MARTIN

CRASHING

through wall of flame
and **OVERTURNING**
CAR AT SPEED

Admission 1/- & 2/-. Children Half-price

SPECIAL CHEAP TRAINS

"CRASHING THROUGH FLAME"

Skid Martin presents.

pits bend he made a hectic effort to get past Reg but the wet surface caused him to spin completely round, leaving Reg to win his first event. The last race of the afternoon was a long distance eight-car eight-lap race. Ron Wills (fifteen yards) was leading when on the last bend of the last lap Walter Mackereth didn't make any mistakes this time and swept around the outside to snatch victory from Wills, with George Turvey, Les White and Frank Chiswell filling the next places.

The drivers from the South of England who had purchased cars and made commitments to race for Wembley and Lea Bridge found themselves rather out on a limb when these tracks ceased to present full time midget car events. Some, such as Les White and Ron Wills, found employment at other tracks. The Lea Bridge drivers could continue their motor racing careers at Crystal Palace, but even here the return of midget car speedway had not proved as successful as had been hoped for. Crystal Palace ran only four home meetings. Their last on 3 September had been against Belle Vue. Drivers needed venues to compete at and spectators needed to see a variety of different drivers other than those drivers based at their 'home' tracks.

With the league now virtually dead, Stoke's next home match was to be a team event against Crystal Palace. As neither league points nor trophy were at stake, the promoters billed this event as a challenge match stating that Crystal Palace were the only team – whether it was the original Lea Bridge team or the team that had been transferred to Crystal Palace – that the Potters had never beaten. Since the last visit of this London team, the Stoke side had been strengthened and the home drivers were confident of gaining revenge for their previous defeats. Stoke fielded the same team that had raced at Coventry. When the Crystal Palace team arrived only four drivers turned up! These were Spike Rhiando, Eddie Hazel, Frank Bullock and Basil deMattos. Nevertheless the meeting went ahead. The management perhaps anticipated a lack of atmosphere in the staging of a mundane challenge match. They decided to liven up the evening's entertainment by introducing a special interval attraction. Skid Martin was to show off his prowess as a stunt driver, he was booked to perform two tricks from his repertoire.

During the match the only time the Potters were ahead was in heat one. Les White and Reg Grice scored a 4-2 heat win and Spike Rhiando came home second. After that Crystal Palace edged ahead, and by heat six they were six points in front, leading twenty-one points to Stoke's fifteen. Up until this heat Crystal Palace had managed to send out two drivers in every race. Whenever possible Crystal Palace drivers had taken their scheduled drives, but when the scheduled drive of an absentee came around his place in the programme was taken by one of the four that had arrived. Obviously this situation could not continue as drivers and cars would tire out. Also the meeting would have become even more farcical because the visiting drivers could have raced up to seven times in the match. So it was that in heats seven and nine Crystal Palace fielded only one driver. Both of these heats were won by the visiting drivers. Spike Rhiando won heat seven and Basil deMattos heat nine. These two wins prevented Stoke from taking advantage of the situation. In the next race, heat ten, the Potters fortunes were not helped when Reg Grice hit the safety fence and turned over. Fortunately, he was uninjured. Previous to this Reg had been going quite well with 1⅔ seconds, each time leading home a member of the opposing side. The match finally ended with a 40-32 points victory to Crystal Palace. The score might have been different had the full complement of Crystal Palace drivers turned up. The four that did race that night were the established 'stars' of the southern scene. Frank Bullock was their top scorer with thirteen, Spike Rhiando eleven; Basil deMattos nine and Eddie Hazel seven. Stoke's highest scorer was Les White with eleven points, his only defeat coming in the last heat when Spike Rhiando beat him in the second fastest time of the night. The rest of the scorers for the Potters were evenly spread from Skid Martin's five points to Joe Wildblood's one. In between these scores came Reg Grice with four and Gene Crowley and Stan Mills with three each. The surprise of the night was Cecil Heath with five points from three races. The local garage owner from Cobridge was improving with every drive and if he continued to improve this way, he would soon be up with the established stars.

The races in the second half of the programme had been curtailed to make way for Skid Martin's stunt performance. For the first of his tricks he attempted to ride a motorcycle through two flaming boards. Whether it was scripted or not Skid brought gasps from the crowd when, after passing through the first board, his machine went out of control; as a result he was catapulted off his motorcycle. He didn't seem too badly shaken and, in true 'Hollywood' style, he quickly remounted his bike and successfully crashed through the second board without mishap. It was then over to four wheels to demonstrate his skills in a motor car. He was attempting to turn over a saloon at high speed. Again he played to the crowd. His first two attempts failed, but he was just getting the feel of the car and the track conditions; on his third attempt he finally rolled the car over, not only that, he had the added bonus of landing the car back on its four wheels. Skid stepped out of the car to the applause of the appreciative supporters. His performance must have impressed, because he was invited to repeat these stunts at Coventry in ten days time.

Concluding the evening's entertainment there were three match races and an eight-lap distance event. All these races were rolling starts. In the first four-lap match race Basil deMattos defeated Gene Crowley. The next two match races were over three laps, in the first Cecil Heath sensationally beat Frank Bullock in a time that was a new three-lap rolling start track record! Cecil didn't have long to savour the fame of holding one of Sun Street records because in the next three-lap match race, Les White beat Spike Rhiando, knocking a further four tenths off Cecils time to leave the new track record at 57.8 seconds. The disappointment of seeing his record broken was short-lived. In the long distance race Cecil triumphed once again. Due to his novice status he had been given twenty-five-yard start. The form he had been showing meant that nobody was going to get near to him. He raced away from the field to win from Eddie Hazel and Frank Bullock, who had started on the fifteen-yard mark.

Traditionally, the end of the season was the time when the various championships, both individual and team, reached their climax and the winners honoured. The brave attempt to establish a Speedway Car League along the same very successful lines as motorcycle speedway failed to materialise. Only Stoke and Coventry had been able to fulfil all their home league commitments. In late August Belle Vue had to call a halt to full midget car meetings, their last full car meeting being the Palatine Trophy on 31 August. This was because the bike riders threatened the management with an ultimatum; either bikes or cars! The damage done to the track by the cars could not be so easily or as thoroughly repaired after car meetings as they could after bike meetings. The speedway riders were a powerful lobby. Earlier they had flexed their muscles when they threatened to go on strike over clubs bringing in too many 'foreign' riders to race in this country. Such was their power and influence that the promoters gave in to their demands. The riders' ultimatums were once again met, which resulted in no more full midget car meetings at Belle Vue, which left Belle Vue with incomplete home league fixtures. A similar and more serious blow to the league occurred earlier at Wembley. Sharing the stadium with bikes threw up a series of problems and the late start to the season hadn't helped. Drivers and cars were given the opportunity to get the 'feel' of the track in special races put on during the second half of the motorcycle speedway meetings. When the cars finally had a meeting to themselves, an individual event for the 'Wembley Gold Cup' (won by Spike Rhiando), members of the motorcycle speedway team came to the conclusion that the cars altered the condition of the track and compromised their safety. They forced the Wembley management to abandon further car meetings. The Wembley team only managed to complete five league matches, all of them raced away from home. The Lea Bridge/Crystal Palace venture folded, it was said, due to lack of support. Only four meetings were held at Crystal Palace after their transfer from Lea Bridge. Of these, only one of them was a league match and this they lost against visitors Belle Vue. The governing body needed to salvage some credence from the setting up of the league and those interested in the sport needed to know where the league now stood. The Board of Control decided that '...owing to the lateness of the season and the impossibility of Wembley and Crystal Palace holding their remaining home fixtures the Board of Control have decided to bring the league to a close naming Coventry premiers for the 1938 season, with Stoke as runners-up. If both these teams were awarded full points for their outstanding matches home and away, with points already gained, that is how the table would finish.' Making the best of the situation Coventry and Stoke followers, management, fans and press alike, realised that this was the best that could be done in the circumstances and accepted this outcome. The final published league table read thus:

	Played	Won	Lost	Drawn	For	Against	Points
Coventry	12	9	3	0	512	346	18
Stoke	11	7	3	1	404	383	15
Crystal Palace/Lea Bridge	8	3	4	1	273½	303½	7
Belle Vue	10	2	8	0	297	414	4
Wembley	5	1	4	0	158½	200½	2

A certain amount of latitude is evident in the make-up of this last league table. It appears that Stoke's abandoned league match against Belle Vue on 11 August was included in the results, with Stoke being awarded the two points for the league win. There may have been other anomalies with this final league table, particularly with the scores for and against, but this didn't matter as only Stoke and Coventry were left presenting serious car meetings. The speedway tracks at Norwich and Bristol ran meetings for cars but these meetings were put on when their respective motorcycle speedway teams were otherwise engaged. No one was going to challenge the league statistics simply because the compilers of these statistics were accountable to no one. All that mattered was that the fans of Stoke and Coventry remained happy and committed to car speedway.

In spite of their late start Stoke had done very well and promoters and fans were delighted with the runners up position. Having settled team honours it was time to settle individual honours. Like followers of any sport, fans want to know who is the best. The Control Board decided that instead of just a one-off meeting to decide who was the individual champion they would hold three meetings; one at Coventry followed by meetings at Stoke and Belle Vue. The Board was hoping that Mr Spence of Belle Vue could be persuaded to run one more individual event. The formula for each event was to be the same at each track with sixteen drivers over twenty heats where each driver met one another once. The points scored by each driver at each event were to be added up and the highest scorer was to be declared the winner. It was left to the Board as to who the lucky sixteen drivers would be. To give added interest, and give those drivers lower down the points scale, something to aim for, the racing numbers for the 1939 season were to be decided on what position you finished in the championship. So not only were the top drivers after the number one logo, but others wanted as low a number as possible.

One driver who was determined to be nominated and drive in the championship was Ted Poole. Having travelled halfway across the world, he wanted to show the British just how good he was. Now that his shoulder and arm were out of plaster and the strength was coming back into his muscles he was out on the Sun Street track. Not only was he testing out his fitness but also trying to impress the officials charged with the selection procedure that he was good enough to be nominated for the championship. When the list was announced for the first round, which was to take place at Coventry on Sunday 25 September, Ted's name was not included. Despite his determination to race, his injuries had not sufficiently healed and, rather than risk further strain to his shoulder, he decided it would be more sensible if he didn't race. Another noticeable name missing from the list of nominees was that of Spike Rhiando who had decided not to race for a while.

Walter Mackereth sitting in his No. 51 car.

Walter Mackereth had won the first round at Coventry. From a Stoke fan's point of view the highlight of the meeting was the outstanding performance of Stan Mills. He had finished the afternoon in third place with twelve points. His best race was in heat fourteen, when he beat his team captain, Les White, in a time of 79.6 seconds, which broke the four-lap, clutch start, Coventry track record. This performance was achieved, not in his own car, but in the spare track car that the Stoke management took along to the meeting just in case any of their drivers hit mechanical trouble. Stan's track record was short-lived. Only three races later Walter Mackereth lowered it even further to 79 seconds. Mackereth's fast time was due, in no small part, to the fact that Stan Mills was right on his tail and pushed him all the way.

Four days later, on Thursday 29 September, the drivers met again for the second round at Sun Street. The fourteen other drivers who carried their scores forward to the Stoke round were: runner-up at Coventry Ron Wills with fourteen; Johnny Young, Bill Reynolds and Frank Chiswell, all on eleven points, followed by George Turvey and Val Atkinson with eight points. A disappointment for the Stoke camp had been Les White's low score of seven points, the same as Buster Bladon. Another below par performance had been that of Basil deMattos with six points. Also well down the score sheet had been the Stoke pair, Skid Martin and Gene Crowley, who both only managed to score three points each. Eddie Hazel had two, Belle Vue's Charlie Pashley one and Jimmy Raines with zero were the other competitors.

All of the above, with the exception of Charlie Pashley who was replaced by Frank Marsh, arrived at Sun Street for the next round. The meeting was not a good night for Stoke supporters, as they only had one of their team members featured in the top ten points scorers. Stan Mills was expected to do well after his good performance at Coventry. After his second drive in heat eight he had to pull out of the meeting when his car developed serious mechanical problems. Obviously this was a great disappointment to the locals. In his first race, heat two, which he easily won, Stan had put up the second fastest time of the night in 78.4 seconds. The fastest time, 78 seconds dead, set by Walter Mackereth, was in heat one when he defeated Les White. Apart from Stan Mills' heat win, the only other Stoke team member to win a race was Les White. This he did twice, in heats fourteen and eighteen. These two victories, however, only pushed his points total for the evening to nine, which was the same as Ron Wills, both drivers finishing in joint fifth place. The top honours were shared evenly between Walter Mackereth, Frank Chiswell and Bill Reynolds, who all scored fourteen points. The overall leader of the competition, Walter Mackereth, was beaten in heat seventeen by Bill Reynolds.

'Bronco' Bill Reynolds was one of the new breed of young up-and-coming drivers who were to leave their mark on the midget car scene. It was not in this country that Bill was to achieve success, but on the other side of the world in Australia. During the winter of 1938/39 Bill took his Skirrow down-under and never returned. He settled in Australia and won their version of the Midget Car World Championship several times. He sensationally defeated the locals in 1939, he repeated the feat in 1941, despite a dispute over lap scoring. After a lengthy retirement he made a comeback in 1956. In that year he won the Australian Speedcar Championship and finished fourth in the World Championship. Two years later, 1958, he again was crowned World Champion. When he finally hung up his crash helmet, he further enhanced his reputation by becoming the resident announcer at the Sydney Showground.

Bill Reynolds had lost his chance of topping the score sheet in heat four when he finished second behind Frank Chiswell. Frank always went well at Sun Street, but he too was to lose his opportunity of winning the event when he finished second behind Walter Mackereth in heat eleven. Both Gene Crowley and Skid Martin had poor scores. Skid Martin, with four, was Stoke's second highest scorer, Gene Crowley failed to score any points at all. The competition had been dominated by Coventry drivers Val Atkinson, Ron Wills (now Coventry-based) and Johnny Young who were the next highest scorers with eleven, nine and seven points respectively. Basil deMattos and Frank Marsh also scored seven. Of the rest of the competitors George Turvey scored six, which included a win in heat three. Coventry's other representative, Buster Bladon scored five which left Eddie Hazel with three. Jimmy Raines failed to score.

Belle Vue's 1938 motorcycle speedway season was to end on Saturday 15 October and this left just two weeks in which to squeeze in the final round of the British Championship. It is evident that talks between those interested in promoting the cause of midget car speedway and Mr Spence, the Belle Vue promoter, broke down as the proposed third and final round never took place. This state of affairs meant that Walter Mackereth with a combined total of twenty-nine points was

Bill Reynolds'
No.78 taking the
lead at Sydney.

the British Champion, Bill Reynolds and Frank Chiswell were joint runners-up with twenty-five points. This should have meant that the following season Walter Mackereth was to carry the coveted number one. Once again, well meaning plans for midget car speedway failed to materialise. Those drivers that continued to race in 1939 carried the numbers that had been allocated to them for the 1938 season.

The following evening the supporters club held their very successful ball at the Grand Hotel, Hanley. With only a few weeks to go before the end of the season, locals continued to show an interest in taking up midget car speedway. Already Cecil Heath and Reg Grice had developed into competent short-circuit oval racers. Other locals who had seen the progress of these two came forward. One such local was Hal Palfreyman of Birches Head. Hal had purchased and taken delivery of the car that Stan Mills had been driving. Another local wishing to try his hand was Chas Bates who came from Clayton; Chas had purchased the Skirrow that the Stoke promotion had used as their track spare. Now that the track was in a much better shape the promoters were once again considering holding trials for prospective drivers. In the pre-war world of motor racing, midget car speedway was unique in so much as background, class, position and financial circumstance was no barrier to those interested in taking up this form of motor racing. A special night was to be laid aside for anyone interested and all applications would be considered. The only financial outlay for those wishing to take part was a small charge to cover fuel and oil.

As the season drew to a close the Control Board and the promoters had to find new competitions to satisfy drivers and fans. The league had been wound up, the individual champion decided; all that was left was to have a cup competition, with a final on a home and away leg. The problem was that there were only two tracks left running full midget car meetings and they were Stoke and Coventry. Coventry only had two more scheduled meetings left; Sundays 2 and 9 October. On 2 October they had defeated a Crystal Palace team in what was advertised as a National Cup competition. In so doing they were to meet Stoke in the final of this hastily thought-up, end-of-season affair. Instead of the usual league format of twelve heats, an extra six races were added to the match. This meant that drivers had six scheduled drives. There were no surprises or changes to the Coventry team but there was a different story for the Potters. At the start of the season Stoke had struggled to put together a viable team, having to make up their side with several 'guest' drivers. Now, instead of searching around to make up the side, it was now a case of who to leave out, especially now that Lane White had recovered from his broken arm and was ready to resume his promising career. There was also the choice between local drivers, Reg Grice and Cecil Heath, which was compounded even more by Cecil's continued improvement. It was finally decided that the team would be: Les White and Cecil Heath, Lane White and Gene Crowley, Stan Mills and Joe Wildblood, with Reg Grice nominated as reserve. The shock omission was Skid Martin; this was the first time that Skid had not been selected for the Stoke team. No reason was given as to why it was decided to rest him from the side. Perhaps Skid's other profession of stunt driver was taking precedence? Just four days previous he had been performing at the Coventry track, once again rolling a saloon car completely over; only this time it proved much more difficult as it was a soaking wet Sunday afternoon. Skid had several attempts at performing this stunt because he was unable to get his car up to the necessary speed on the greasy surface.

Up until heat eight this cup match was very close, with the Potters just two points in front. A first and a second place in heats two and four by Lane White showed that his accident had not affected his driving skills or confidence. In heat nine, Val Atkinson and Frank Chiswell pushed Lane down to third place and this now put the 'Bees' two points ahead. In the next race Walter Mackereth beat his old rival Les White, with Buster Bladon third. The Potters were beginning to slip behind; a fight back was needed. In heat eleven, Lane White and Joe Wildblood faced Johnny Young and Val Atkinson. Fired up by the need to pull back the deficit, Lane was a little too over-enthusiastic and hit the safety fence rather hard. This accident shook him up rather badly and sufficiently enough for him to take no further part in the rest of the meeting. Also involved in Lane's crash was Johnny Young. His car had overturned and rolled completely over. Johnny was thrown out of his car and, fortunately, he escaped serious injury, and he too was rather shaken up and took no further part in the meeting. Val Atkinson won the rerun and this pushed Stoke further behind. With Lane White now out of the meeting, the only Stoke drivers capable of beating Coventry's top drivers were Les White and Stan Mills. Stan had won his first four races, and this included a great victory over Walter Mackereth in heat seven, but he was unable to do anything about Val Atkinson and Ron Wills in heat fourteen. By then Coventry had gained a nine-point advantage and Stan's defeat had pushed the Potters further behind. In the latter stages Stoke tried to pull back the points by sending out Les White in the last four races! Two of which were his scheduled drives, the other two he replaced his fellow team members. Although he won two races and finished second twice, Stoke were unable to prevent Coventry winning by 58 points to 47. Stoke now had the impossible task of pulling back eleven points on a track where Coventry had never been defeated. Of the forty-seven points scored by Stoke, Les White and Stan Mills had gained thirty-six of them. Les had raced to twenty points from eight starts and Stan, sixteen from six starts. Apart from Lane White, who scored six from three starts, the rest of the team were nowhere. The only points they gained were 'gifted' to them when either a Coventry or Stoke driver failed to finish. Joe Wildblood scored three; Gene Crowley and Cecil Heath one point each. Coventry scorers were much more consistent; Mackereth seventeen, Atkinson fifteen, Young and Bladon six each and finally Wills with five points showed their strength in depth.

For the return leg on the following Sunday Skid Martin was back in the side, Cecil Heath having to make way for his return. This Stoke line-up was just about the strongest team they could field. A close return match was anticipated, with the Coventry fans looking forward to renewing their rivalry with the travelling Stoke supporters. Due to the lateness of the motor racing season and the fact that, unlike Sun Street, the Brandon Stadium was devoid of floodlighting, the start of the meeting was to begin earlier than normal. The Stoke team arrived late! Whether they were not told about this or they forgot is not known, but this unfortunate oversight was just the beginning of an eventful afternoon. To compound the problems even further, half the Potters' cars failed to arrive; it looked like the meeting would be a walkover for the Coventry Bees.

Eventually the meeting got under way with the Stoke drivers agreeing to beg or borrow cars from wherever they could. The Potters pulled back some of the points deficit straight away when Les White won the opening heat. In fact, Les had been the only finisher in this opening race; Walter Mackereth, Buster Bladon and Skid Martin had all collided with one another at the Rugby bend. So badly damaged were Mackereth's and Martin's cars that neither was able to take to the track again. Now they both had to borrow cars belonging to their team-mates. The Potters never managed to pull back the deficit. One person who stood out for the Stoke side was Stan Mills. Stan's regular mount had been one of the cars that had failed to turn up and, throughout the meeting, he had been driving the Stoke team's track spare. This car was regularly taken to both home and away matches to cover incidents like this. Stan drove this car to victory three times in the first five races. So good was this driver–car combination that in heat five Stan lowered the track record to 78.2 seconds knocking 0.8 seconds off Walter Mackereth's old track record. This worked out at an average speed of 41.96mph. Not only did Stan lower the track record in heat five but he was also under Mackereth's old track record in heats eight and eleven. Maybe it was because the car was not his own that he threw caution to the wind and drove so boldly. The spare car was out in nearly every race. In heat ten Les White had driven it to victory and in this race too White was under Mackereth's old track record. There is an old adage in speedway that a motor always goes well before it blows up! Eventually of course the inevitable happened in heat twelve. With Stan Mills at the wheel, the engine expired and the Potters were now even more short of competitive cars. Because of the delayed start, missing cars and accidents, time was running out and darkness was approaching. Only two more races were completed before the meeting had to be abandoned, the score standing at 50 points to Coventry and 29 to Stoke. Stan Mills had scored sixteen points from six starts; Les White only had three starts and had scored eight points. For the rest of the Stoke team: Gene Crowley scored

Far left: League champions Coventry 'Bees'. From left to right: Frank Chiswell, George Turvey, Walter Mackereth (sitting in Frank Chiswell's car) Val Atkinson, Johnny Young and Buster Bladon. (Courtesy of Roy Chiswell)

Left: Les Foster.

three, Joe Wildblood and Lane White one point each and Skid Martin failed to score. The aggregate scores after fourteen heats were 108 points to 76 points in favour of Coventry. So, even if the competition had gone to the full eighteen races and the Potters, by a miracle, had won every heat, they could not have overhauled Coventry. Consequently, Coventry were declared the winners. With the light almost gone the victorious Coventry side did a lap of honour with their captain Walter Mackereth parading the winners' trophy.

The 1938 season at Sun Street ended on Thursday 13 October. For this last meeting it was decided to continue with the successful team format. This last meeting was advertised as a 'Triangular Teams Match' where the Stoke team were to compete against a combined Coventry and Crystal Palace side. In addition to the team racing there was to be six lap races for the Tony Pendrill trophy. The most anticipated event of the evening was neither of these but a special series of match races. It was not the usual challenge between established stars or regular Stoke drivers but between two local lads who had been regular visitors to Sun Street. One was the already mentioned Hal Palfryman and the other was Les Foster. Hal was a twenty-eight-year-old electrician from Birches Head. The car that he had purchased was kept at the garage of his friend Cecil Heath. Hal had had a few laps around the Sun Street track and felt he was ready to have a serious attempt at midget car racing. His opponent, Les Foster, was a couple of years younger. Les came from a farming family who lived at Belverdere Farm, Barlaston. He was a well-known local character, described by those who knew him as 'loveable rogue'. In keeping with his character, he had challenged Hal to a match race. Both drivers had agreed to put down £25 each with the winner walking away with £50. This was quite a substantial amount in 1938. Although Les did not, as yet, own his own car, he had driven a few laps during track trials. The car he was to use in the match race had been loaned to him by his friend, Reg Grice.

This last meeting of the season was run under rather poor conditions. The track was greasy due to the recent rains that had swept the Potteries. One absentee from the Stoke side was Lane White who had decided to give this last meeting a miss. The combined team was very strong and contained the Coventry drivers Walter Mackereth, Val Atkinson, Frank Chiswell and the 'on loan' Ron Wills. To these were added Crystal Palace's Frank Bullock and Eddie Hazel. Because of the conditions, the racing and the times were very slow, with drivers having great difficulty keeping their cars on the track. No one was taking the slightest risks on the bends. It was rather an anti-climax to the end of the season for Stoke supporters as their team was always chasing the opposition, eventually losing heavily by 25 points to the visitors 47. Stoke's only heat winner was Les White in heat six. He finished the meeting with two more second places, ending the night as the Potters' highest scorer with seven. Skid Martin had 2⅓ seconds for five points, even Stan Mills found the going not at all to his liking only managing to score four points. As for the rest of the team, Gene Crowley scored four, Cecil Heath and reserve Reg Grice won two apiece and Joe Wildblood gained one third place for a solitary point. Walter Mackereth was, as usual, brilliant. No matter what the conditions, he was way ahead of the opposition, going through the challenge match unbeaten. Eddie Hazel only matched his slowest winning time of 85 seconds in heat eleven when the track was drying out. Frank Chiswell, with eleven, was the visitors' next highest scorer followed by Ron Wills with eight, Val Atkinson with seven, Eddie Hazel with five, and finally Frank Bullock with four.

It was now time for the first of the three match races. After all the preparation and build up, the event fizzled out. Hal Palfryman was ready to go, but for Les Foster it turned out to be a great disappointment. He had to pull out because the car he was to borrow developed engine trouble and he was not able to compete.

Rounding off the night and the season was to be two qualifying heats and a final for the Tony Pendrill Trophy. All the races were over six laps. Joining the drivers from the previous challenge match was Bill Reynolds who had made the trip up from London just to compete in this, the last event of 1938. Qualifying from the first heat were Walter Mackereth and Bill Reynolds. In the second heat Val Atkinson and Les White made their way into the final. The final was Bill's last performance in this country before he set sail for Australia. In true romantic style, Bill won the final, thus gaining revenge over Walter Mackereth who had beaten him in the first heat.

Although this was the last meeting of the midget car season for 1938 it was not the last time that the people of the Potteries could watch midget car speedway. The following Thursday, Sun Street Stadium was the venue for a visit from one of the pre-war period's most famous stunt shows. Putt Mossman was in town to present his famous Rodeo and Speedway Circus. With typical American flair, Putt went through his various motorcycle tricks, which included crashing through a blazing board wall, and his famed ladder walk, whereby he would attempt to climb up one side of a ladder and down the other side whilst balancing the motorcycle to which it was attached. The climax of the evening was when he rode his motorcycle down a 1ft-wide ramp that had been attached to the top of the spectator terracing. At the end of the ramp, a member of the stunt team, sometimes his wife, would lie full length on the ground. All this was to be done blindfolded! On the programme were a couple of midget car performances. Putt was no stranger to the world of midget car racing as he and Bob Deihl, a member of his stunt team, had competed in the midget car 'World Championship' at Hackney Wick in August 1936.

In the first of the midget car demonstrations Putt raced his speedway bike against a midget car driven by none other than Spike Rhiando. The car easily won as Spike raced around the out side of the track this gave the bike more room: the outside line on this occasion proving to be the faster line. The second car event was a special match race. To make up for the disappointment of the previous week, Les Foster was given the chance to prove what he could do; he was to race against Putt Mossman himself. Mossman, who, it was said, drove a more powerful car, won the race. Foster put up a surprisingly good race and was later complemented by Mossman on his performance. The car that Spike Rhiando and Putt Mossman drove was a Skirrow owned by the stunt team. This car was later taken on tour by Mossman to Australia where it was later raced by Cec Garland, one of Australia's top speedway car and bike racers.

The brief three months of motor racing at Sun Street was now over, spectators, drivers, and management were looking forward with enthusiasm to 1939. From a team-building point of view things looked good; Stoke had managed to put together a reasonable set of drivers. Early in the season they had to make up their team with the dubious practice of fielding drivers with false names, including 'Les Black', 'Jimmy deMattos' and 'Jock Fergusson'. As racing became more established and more drivers came forward, this practice of hoodwinking the public stopped. If for 1939, their 'loaned' drivers, Les White and Stan Mills, returned to their parent tracks, the Potters would still be able to field a team of their own. The loss of their two star drivers, Squib Burton and Ted Poole, had been overcome by the introduction of newcomers to the sport. Up until his injury, Lane White had a meteoric rise culminating in his performances in the Tommy Sulman trophy and his great performance in the North v South Test Match at Crystal Palace. Locals Reg Grice and Cecil Heath too had shown great promise. At the beginning of their careers, Grice was perhaps the better of the two but Cecil Heath was now developing into a much more accomplished all-round performer. With the close season in front of them, there was plenty of time for novices Hal Palfryman, Les Foster, and Chas Bates to acquire the necessary skills of broad siding four-wheel-drive racing cars around the tight and dangerous speedway circuits.

As for the future of midget car speedway, things were looking decidedly healthy. Besides the tracks that had taken part in the league, full car meetings had taken place at Norwich, Leeds, Edinburgh, Hackney Wick, and Bristol. In all there had been at least seventy meetings run exclusively for midget cars. An extremely healthy number and one that kept the professional drivers busy all season. Mr Guy Hopkins, the secretary of the N.A.S.C.R.C. (the governing body), was upbeat about the sport's future. He claimed that he had already received enquiries from several parts of the country to run midget car speedway. He was confidently predicting that there would be seven teams competing in the league for the 1939 season.

seven

Cobridge
Capers

On Thursday 20 April 1939, once again four competitors broadsided into the first bend at Sun Street Stadium, sending up showers of black cinders as they diced for position on the first lap. At the end of four hectic laps, Stoke led Belle Vue by four points to two. Ted Bravery had crossed the line in 81.4 seconds finishing ahead of E. Price and Fred Tuck. If these names seemed unfamiliar to the midget car fan then this was because the four protagonists were not midget car drivers but motorcycle speedway riders.

During the winter months, the rights to run motor sport at the stadium had changed hands. The owners of the stadium had decided to accept the offer put forward by a local consortium to run motorcycle speedway whereby Stoke were to operate in the Second Division of the Speedway National League. The new promoters had close links with Belle Vue, Manchester, with many of the Stoke riders racing for Belle Vue's reserve team. For the people of the Potteries, competitive midget car speedway was in the doldrums.

It was not only the Potteries that found themselves bereft of midget car speedway but other parts of the country too. The 1938 season had ended on a high note of optimism, the governing body's over-enthusiastic plans for 1939 coming to nought. None of the expected new ventures opened and those speedway tracks that had run car meetings found themselves pressured again by the bike riders not to allow cars to cut up the racing surface. Australian riders led a lot of this pressure. This pressure may have been due to the self-preservation of the speedway riders seeing their livelihood being taken away from them. Motorcycle speedway had been losing ground to car speedway in Australia. Car speedway was now becoming the number one form of oval racing down-under. Even Frank Arthur, an Australian speedway promoter, who had been against the cars, now found himself a leading champion of the Car speedway cause.

The English speedway promoters didn't completely freeze out the cars as they put on a few car races after the bikes had finished as extra second-half attractions. The few car races that took place didn't cause too many problems to the track surface, giving track maintenance crews an easier time to put the track back to racing requirements. This compromise of presenting a few car races after the bikes kept faith with the drivers and fans who wished to see the midget cars. If the car fans of the Potteries had been missing the excitement of the midget cars then they had to travel to other parts of the country to witness car speedway racing.

With the demise of midget car speedway racing in Stoke, the drivers had to decide about their futures. Ted Poole returned to his native Australia, his early injury problems spoiling his trip to England. Skid Martin also left these shores and he headed off to South Africa with his fellow stunt driver Reg Kavanagh. There, the two of them toured that country with a group of stunt drivers performing at various stadiums. The White brothers, Stan Mills and Gene Crowley continued to put in appearances at other tracks, although it was not until late May that Les White resumed racing as he had been recovering from an operation. Joe Wildblood and Cecil Heath now found themselves at Coventry. Although neither of them found a place in the Coventry team, they did, however, compete regularly at Brandon throughout the beginning of the 1939 season. The two new, local 'late comers' to the sport, Hal Palfryman and Les Foster continued their efforts to become

There was not much thought for spectator safety in the late 1930s as this photograph shows. Spectators could get right up to the action; one child is seen sitting on the safety fence dangling his legs over the track! (Courtesy of Bob Light)

recognised drivers. Both began to have second-half drives, again at Coventry. Reg Grice did not bother to continue racing, having sold off his equipment to Les Foster.

The first full midget car speedway meeting of 1939 was at Coventry on 9 April. It was a best pair's event, which was won by George Turvey and Charlie Pashley. If any followers of the sport from the Potteries attended that day then they would have seen Cecil Heath finish joint second with his partner Val Atkinson. As the season progressed, Cecil Heath's driving became a revelation. Several early season good performances culminated in being chosen to drive for the North in a revamp of the North v South series. The other Potteries-based drivers were now getting regular racing experience. Les Foster was beginning to pick up a few second and third places in second-half events. The local Coventry Press appreciated his determination and enthusiasm, when in a mid-June meeting his efforts earned him the title of the unluckiest driver of the day. Les had come into the meeting as a substitute for Eric Worswick. In Les's first race, he hit the fence when well in the lead. In his next race, his car spun completely round on the first lap, he repeated

A 1939 Coventry Supporters' Badge. (Courtesy of Ian Sommerville)

Cecil Heath passes on the inside as a fellow competitor over-cooks it on a bend at Coventry's Brandon track. (Courtesy of Brian Heath)

this performance in his next race. Apparently, the damage to the car sustained in his first race had badly affected the car's handling and he had to pull out of his final drive. Hal Palfryman's first taste of serious competitive racing came in late May, when he was given a three-lap match race against Coventry newcomer Doug Mogdridge, which Mogdridge won in 67 seconds.

Five weeks after the opening motorcycle speedway meeting at Sun Street, car fans' interests were rekindled as the speedway promoters at Hanley decided to include midget cars in the second half of the programme after Stoke's National Trophy speedway match against Hackney Wick. The inclusion of cars on the programme had come about because of pressure from spectators who had previously enjoyed the spectacle of the cars. As well as enjoying the bikes, they wanted to see the cars back. On Saturday 20 May, an advert in the local newspaper announced that Walter Mackereth was to race Spike Rhiando in a series of match races over six laps. Not only were these two stars to compete but also local drivers Les Foster, Hal Palfryman and Chas Bates were to try and see who was the best local newcomer – an event that had ended in frustration at the last car meeting of the 1938 season. There was a last-minute hitch with the star match race as Walter Mackereth had an important business commitment to attend to and was unable to race. On the Wednesday, a replacement had been found, Stoke's ex-captain Les White was to take up the challenge. This last-minute change of plan came too late to alter the advertising copy that had been sent out. As late as the Thursday of the meeting the *Evening Sentinel* was still advertising the fact that the match race was to be between Mackereth and Rhiando. The help that the Stoke promotion received from Belle Vue was highlighted in so much as the printing block used to advertise the midget car race was the same as the one used the previous year by the Belle Vue promotion.

Stoke Speedways' car advert using the same image that was used the previous year (1938) to advertise car speedway at Belle Vue.

The match race turned out to be a disappointment; after two laps of close racing, Spike Rhiando's car suffered engine trouble, presenting Les White with an easy victory. The other car event was programmed as 'Potteries own scratch race', it was to be over four laps with a clutch start. This turned out to be a match race between Foster and Palfryman because Harry (Chas) Bates non-started. The race was won by Les Foster whose time of 95.6 seconds was probably the slowest time ever recorded for a four-lap clutch start by a midget car around Sun Street! This was a rather contentious result as Les Foster had been all over the track, including a trip across the grass on the centre green where certain officials were standing. Fortunately, general manager, Jim France, saw Les coming, and swiftly ran out of the way of the erratic Foster.

The inclusion of the midget cars in the programme boosted the crowd's numbers; the local Press reported a record crowd! Whether this was true or not will never be known, as attendance figures were never ever published; the exact number passing through the turnstiles always remained a close secret between stadium owners, promoters, accountants and the Inland Revenue! Although attendance figures were given to the Press these were often exaggerated to boost interest, giving the impression to the public that they too should not miss out on the excitement.

The following week midget cars were again to be part of the programme. Jim France, the general manager, decided to give the cars another chance to prove their worth. The disappointment of the week before or the reported increase in attendance may have had something to do with it. This time Walter Mackereth didn't have any commitments and was booked to race against Les White. Again the two locals Foster and Palfryman were to race one another. This time, however, they were to be joined by ex-Stoke stalwart Joe Wildblood.

Problems again manifested themselves in the 'star' match race. This week the drivers managed three laps before Les White had to pull in with tyre trouble. This was a poor advert for midget car racing; for the second week running the stars had failed to perform.

It was left to the lesser lights to salvage some pride for the car drivers. All managed to finish, with Wildblood winning easily. This time, Hal Palfryman beat Les Foster for the minor places. Rather than just take the start money and walk away, Les White replaced his tyre and the match race was back on. The re-run was over three laps. In a 'skilfully contested duel,' Mackereth just won.

For the following week, the Stoke programme of Thursday 1 June proclaimed 'Colossal Car Races between World Famous Drivers'. It was to be the highlight of the second half of the motorcycle speedway match between Stoke and Newcastle. However, the Stoke promoters were not happy with the entertainment that the added attraction midget car racing was supposed to bring.

The expense of staging the car event did not appear to warrant the extra financial outlay. A statement to that effect was issued the following week; 'the whole of the second half of the programme will be devoted to motorcycles. The manager of the Stadium, Mr J. France, states that the increase in the attendance as a result of the inclusion of car races did not reach expectations and consequently no car events will be included in future motorcycle programmes.' This sudden abandonment of car racing was perhaps, not only due to the mediocre reliability of the cars, but also due to an announcement that appeared in the local Press. On Wednesday

31 May it was confirmed that a new track, about a mile away at nearby Cobridge, was under construction and furthermore it was going to present midget car speedway racing.

The Albion Stadium at Waterloo Road, Cobridge had been renovated as recently as 1932 to accommodate the booming sport of greyhound racing. It was a larger track than Sun Street and had plenty of room for expansion. Work on the track had already begun, local labour being employed on what was designed to be the fastest oval in the country. The track was to be about a quarter of a mile in length, 40ft-wide on the straights, with 60ft-wide sweeping bends. The newly formed company behind this ambitious project went under the name of 'Cobridge Motordrome Ltd'.

One local driver who had been missing from the second-half events at Sun Street was Cecil Heath. Cecil was now an established safe, fast, and competent driver very popular with the Coventry fans and his fellow drivers. Cecil, who had now become hooked on midget car speedway, decided that the people of the Potteries were missing out on motor sport. Cecil's garage was very close to the Albion Stadium and seeing that the site could be developed for midget car speedway, he took the plunge and set up the company to promote motor racing. Together with John Dickenson, of Sneyd Green, they set up the company with a capital of £500. The company was registered with Jordan's Daily Register nominating Cecil as managing director.

Just as drivers Ted Poole and Gene Crowley had been consulted over track preparation at Sun Street, so track development at this new venue was overseen by ex-Stoke favourite Stan Mills. Work progressed well with the construction of the circuit; by mid-June, it was ready for the first cars to try it out. Of course, both Cecil Heath and Stan Mills were the first drivers to christen the track.

Labourers get to grips with the laying of the Cobridge track. The bottle kilns of the Globe Pottery works in the top right-hand corner. (Courtesy of Brian Heath)

Cecil Heath and Joe Wildblood pose for the camera at Cobridge. (Courtesy of Brian Heath)

Everything was ready for the opening night. This was to be on Thursday 29 June. Just quite why this day was chosen is unknown, as the pre-publicity had said that Saturday night was to be the race day. To the independent onlooker this date seemed rather an odd decision, because just down the road the Stoke 'Potters' motorcycle speedway team were racing Hackney Wick in a National League Division Two fixture. To counter this alternative attraction, the Cobridge management needed to put on an evening's entertainment that would not only attract the former followers of the Stoke 'Potters' speedway car team but also attract other spectators looking for alternate motorised forms of entertainment. The growing car ownership of the district made it a good main target area. To encourage motorist to come along car parking was free; the stadium car park was able to accommodate over 500 cars.

To nurture a loyal following the management set about building up a core of supporters who would spread the word about the exciting and entertaining world of midget car speedway. The previous year a well-run supporters club had organised and put on several events for the followers of the sport. Cobridge too followed the same route by setting up a supporters club, a side of the venture that the directors were very keen on.

The first meeting was to be a team event; at the time, this seemed to be the preferred option as opposed to individual events. Because there was no longer any league racing, teams could be made up to represent whatever the promoters thought would attract the public. Naturally, the majority of the Cobridge team was made up of the former drivers who had been based at Sun Street and had been members of the Stoke 'Potters' car speedway Team. As with most team events a nickname was needed and the name chosen was 'The Tigers'. This prevented any confusion with the motorcycle speedway team. When the press talked about 'The Tigers' the public knew it was talking about the car speedway team.

The Cobridge 'Tigers' were captained by Cecil Heath and included ex-Potters Les White, Stan Mills, and Joe Wildblood. The other two ex-Potters, Gene Crowley and Skid Martin, were not available. Skid Martin had not yet returned from South Africa, being due back some time in early July. Manchester's Eric Worswick and George Turvey made up the rest of the 'Tigers'.

For the opening meeting 'The Tigers' were to take on 'The Rest' – a team led by Walter Mackereth and backed up by Johnny Young, Ron Wills, Frank Marsh and, new to Potteries fans, Chas Bennett. Chas had been a regular competitor at Coventry during the 1937 season. He had taken a year off from racing and, during his time away from competition, he had looked after the interests and equipment of Buster Bladon. He was now back and driving better than ever. The final member of the visiting team was none other than Harry Skirrow himself. Over the past year or so Harry had been busy manufacturing his specials and promoting the sport rather than competing. Racing midget cars had been the reason he had become involved in car speedway in the first place; racing competitively had had to take second, or even third, place. His inclusion in the team allowed the Potteries folk to see how well he coped with his disability. The meeting was to be opened by the Haywood Hospital Carnival Queen; she was also on hand to present the trophy for the second-half final, which was a six-car six-lap event.

Also on the programme was a youngster by the name of 'Dare Devil Ken', who was to give a demonstration of his driving skills in a midget car during the interval. Ken was apparently only seven years and ten months old! He had performed previously at Crystal Palace and Lea Bridge and he had featured in a Paramount Newsreel films that had been shot at Coventry in September 1937 when he, if the pre-publicity was to be believed, would have been only six years old.

The team event was over nine heats with each driver having three races. The first race on the new track ended rather ignominiously for Cecil Heath. With all the effort he and his partner had put into bringing midget car racing back to the Potteries, it was a great disappointment that engine failure in the opening heat threatened to put an end to his night's racing. Chas Bennett too failed to finish, leaving just Walter Mackereth to continue where he left off at Sun Street by leading home Les White in a time of 85.6 seconds.

The score ebbed and flowed, the lead changing hands three times during the match. Heat five was one of the closest and best races of the night when Stan Mills defeated Walter Mackereth in a time of 78.8 seconds; that was over 3 seconds faster than any other time recorded on the night. At the end of this heat the 'Tigers' led by seventeen points to twelve. However, in the next two races – heats six and seven, Johnny Young put in a couple of good heat wins, which included beating Les White in the latter race. Young's team mates finished third in both races to give the Rest a lead of twenty-one points to twenty.

The last two races saw maximum points for the visitors; the score finally ending twenty-three points to the 'Tigers' and thirty for the Rest. The delighted winner

Car Speedway

— A T —

COBRIDGE

MOTORDROME

STOKE-ON-TRENT

**Opening Meeting—Thursday, June 29th
at 7-30 p.m.**

Official **3d.** Programme

The Cobridge programme's front cover used the same artwork as was used the previous year for the Sun Street 1938 adverts.

of the last race was Harry Skirrow who showed that, despite his lack of regular competition, he was still capable of turning in a good performance. The Tigers' top scorer was Les White with seven points; Eric Worswick scored six (which included a win over Johnny Young in heat three), George Turvey five and Stan Mills three. From a racing point of view, the two Potteries drivers, Joe Wildblood and Cecil Heath, had an opening night they would rather have forgotten. After seizing his engine in the first race, Cecil managed to borrow a car from a fellow competitor in order to complete his scheduled drives. The only points he scored, two, came in heat four when he came second behind Les White. Joe Wildblood was dogged with punctures and in one race he had two flat tyres. Unfortunately, he failed to score a single point.

For the visiting team it was the Coventry-based drivers who dominated; Johnny Young was the top scorer with eight followed by Walter Mackereth with seven, Ron Wills five, Harry Skirrow four and both Frank Marsh and Chas Bennett three. Bennett's three points came when Walter Mackereth shepherded him home for a five one in heat eight.

After 'Dare Devil Ken' had given his demonstration of broadsiding and Eric Worswick had defeated Gordon Hanstock, in what was termed a 'Bad Luck' race, it was time for the six-lap, six-car races. The qualifiers for the final were, from heat one; Walter Mackereth – once again leading home Les White – and Cecil Heath third. In heat two Chas Bennett won in a time over 11 seconds slower than Mackereth's time in the previous heat! Much 'bumping and boring' taking place, the other two finishers were Eric Worswick and Frank Marsh. In the final there were thrills and spills galore and, on one of the bends, no less than five cars ran into one another. Fortunately, none of the cars overturned and no one was hurt. The race winner was a rather lucky Eric Worswick, whose time was 16.4 seconds slower than Mackereth's heat win. Mackereth really should have won the final. The five car melée early in the race affected his chances of victory when his tyre burst on the last bend.

The first meeting seems to have been a success, the counter attraction of the Stoke v Hackney Wick motorcycle speedway match less than a mile along the A53 did not appear to rob the attendance of too many spectators. The *City Times* reporter claimed that, 'It was evident by the high attendance at the Cobridge Motordrome racing track last night; the midget car racing had been warmly welcomed by the Potteries'. On behalf of the motorcyclists, it is also interesting to note that the *Evening Sentinel* said, 'In spite of a racing counter attraction, the Sun Street speedway maintained an excellent attendance last night'. As to who was telling the truth, only time would tell. After the dilemma of whether to attend the car racing or the bike racing, locals had their minds made up for them. The following Thursday neither venue presented motorised sport. The Potters speedway team were racing away at Sheffield; the 'Tigers' car team were to race Coventry on their scheduled Saturday night.

As with all newly-laid speedway tracks, the racing surface had cut up badly and had to be re-laid for the next meeting, the bends having to be completely replaced. The Saturday race night gave the track staff an extra two days to put things right. So confident were the maintenance crew of the job they had done, that in addition to the normal racing events, solo attempts on the track record were to be made.

With no alternate meeting, a good crowd was expected for the Coventry challenge match. This time the team event was to be over the more familiar twelve-heat formula that had been used the previous season for league racing. Six-car, six-lap scratch races were again to feature in the second half. When plans were first announced for the opening of the motordrome, it was decided that amateur races were to be held. Trials similar to those that had been held at Sun Street were scheduled to take place, details of which were to be given over the public address system and in the official programme. As a precursor to the expected amateur events, one was added to this week's programme.

On the day before the Coventry match those fans who had been undecided whether to watch the cars or the bikes had their minds made up for them when newspaper headlines read 'Stoke Speedway to close' – this of course was the Sun Street venue. The article blamed the closure on 'the poor measure of support which has been accorded the team's home fixtures the deciding decision to resign from the league was made solely because of lack of support.' The promoters claimed they needed a gate of 5,000 to break even. With the closure of Sun Street, support for Cobridge was expected to increase.

The vagaries of the British summer were to manifest themselves on Saturday 7 July. Torrential rain during the day put the meeting in doubt; it was not until 7 p.m., forty-five minutes before the scheduled start, that it was decided to call off the meeting and re-schedule it for the following Saturday.

Cecil Heath, Les White, Stan Mills, and Joe Wildblood were again to drive for the 'Tigers', this time they were joined by Frank Marsh and Gene Crowley, who was making a welcome return to the Potteries. The Coventry team had the same driver line-up that had contested the opening meeting under the title of 'The Rest'! The only difference was that Val Atkinson drove in place of Frank Marsh. This seemed a little unimaginative, if the venue was to succeed then more variety would surely be needed for later meetings.

Looking ahead, the management wanted to develop the venue for other sports, and a call went out to cycle clubs inviting them to stage events there. This was something that Coventry had been doing that year.

The second car meeting of the season saw Cobridge Tigers race to a 39–33 victory. Although Les White was undefeated in his four races, scoring a maximum twelve points, it was the great driving of Cecil Heath that shone out. In less than twelve months, he was now defeating much more experienced drivers.

In the team event he won two races and finished second twice to give him the best result of his career; his only defeats being at the hands of Walter Mackereth in heat one and Val Atkinson in heat four. Up until heat five, the score had been even, with fifteen points to each side, and after that the Coventry side never had a heat winner except in heat eleven when Mackereth won from Crowley and Wills. Stan Mills too had a good night winning his first three races, to score nine points. The 'Tigers' had no other heat winners. Returnee Gene Crowley had five drives in the match and registered five points. Frank Marsh had two third places, two points, and Joe Wildblood one point. Only Walter Mackereth, with eleven points from five drives, and Val Atkinson, eight points, scored heat wins for Coventry. Their next highest scorer was Chas Bennett had six. Johnny Young and Harry Skirrow had a poor night's racing, and both only scored three points each. Ron Wills too was below par with two third places. With the track now in much better shape than it was for the opening meeting, solo attempts on the track record were made. It was no surprise to see Walter Mackereth register the fastest time of 78.6 seconds for a four-lap rolling start.

The amateur race that had been added to the programme threw up not only new talent wanting to break into midget car speedway but also a fresh approach to midget car design. Although the race was won by L.O. Breeze of Manchester with Wilf Mellor of Oldham coming second, it was Gordon Hanstock who had finished in third place that drew most attention. Gordon was only twenty-four and had managed to design and build his own car. His only previous midget car racing experience had been at Cobridge's opening meeting and one second-half

An early photograph of Frank Marsh sitting in his Elto. Note the crude roll bar. This he later removed because it was too heavy.

race at Coventry. He hailed from Worksop and, like Harry Skirrow, he had a natural engineering flair. The car he created was similar to the Skirrow Special, in so much as it had four-wheel-drive, but power came from two J.A.P. speedway engines, both mounted in the front of the car; one engine driving the front wheels and the other driving the rear. This machine was chain driven. After the war Gordon's engineering skills were channelled into Hanstock Engineering, the family's engineering concern, where they produced several innovative products for the motor trade.

Walter Mackereth won the climax of the evening – a six-car race over six laps. This made up for the disappointment of missing out in the final, sixteen days previously. A rejuvenated Gene Crowley was second and Johnny Young third. The other competitors who made it through to the final were Val Atkinson, Frank Marsh, and Joe Wildblood. One name missing from this final was Les White. After his four wins in the team event, Les should have easily made it through to the final. However, a big end went in the qualifying heat, which prevented his progress to the final.

The midget car scene during 1939 was nowhere near as strong as it had been the previous year. The anticipated explosion in car racing had not materialised. Jimmy Baxter and his followers had confidently expected midget car speedway to eclipse motorcycle speedway. This at the time might not be as exaggerated as it might at first seem. During the late 1930s motoring was reaching out to a wider public. Morris, Ford and Austin were all manufacturing small cars that were not beyond the reach of the general public. The interest in the motor car, it was hoped, would reflect in the public's demand to see car racing. In fact, The Albion Stadium, Cobridge, was advertised as a place where motorists met. Another area that fuelled the optimism for midget car racing was what was happening in Australia, the birthplace of motorcycle speedway. Reports coming out of Australia claimed that motorcycle speedway was on the way out and dying a natural death as more and more competitors turned to midget car speedway. Australian presentation of the sport was in complete contrast to this country. Because of the vast distances between cities, team racing, on a national basis, was out of the question. Individual events were the norm with lots of cars over as many as thirty laps. These car feature events were now pushing the bikes out of the limelight and midget cars were now the main attraction.

There had been a two-way exchange of drivers between Britain and Australia. Tommy Sulman and Ted Poole had come to these shores to race. Even as late as 1939, Cec Garland, another Antipodean, visited this country. Cec never had the opportunity to race at Cobridge; he was due to make his debut at Coventry on Sunday 9 July but the night before, he broke his leg whilst racing bikes up at Glasgow's White City Stadium. A few English drivers had already visited Australia, Jean Revelle, and Bill Reynolds staying there after their winter trips. The go-ahead Australian promoters were always keen to improve their presentations and seeing that there were plenty of capable midget car drivers in Britain, they decided to invite over a team of English drivers. Although events in Europe were to overtake these plans, several drivers were keen on the trip and jumped at the opportunity to sample a different racing atmosphere and culture. One of the prospective 'emigrants' was Hanley's Hal Palfryman. Having not yet broken into the top flight of racing, ever-improving Hal felt that the experience of racing in Australia would improve his career. Another who was keen to go was Harry Skirrow. Harry had little to prove as a racer – his previous motorcycle and car exploits spoke for themselves, it was Harry's natural engineering ability and entrepreneurial flair that attracted him to sign up for the trip. There would have been many opportunities to produce and market his brilliant 'Skirrow' special, 99 per cent of the midget racing cars in Australia being 'back yard' specials. Though whether he would have been able to continue manufacturing his four-wheel-drive version of the car in Australia is debatable. In later years the four-wheel-drive was banned in Australia and the USA. The authorities there claimed that these cars were far too dangerous. The controversy centred on the drive mechanism. When the front wheels touched another car or the safety fence, these cars had a dramatic tendency to climb up and over them. The war sadly preventing this trip from taking place.

The next meeting scheduled to take place at the motordrome was the 'All England Championship.' The year before the controlling body had tried to organize an event worthy of the title with three individual rounds, but this ended

Cec Garland at Sydney driving the Skirrow Special that Putt Mossman had taken over to Australia the previous winter. In 1938 Cec finished second in this car to Paul Swedberg in the Australian version of the World Championship.

up with just two rounds. Now, in 1939 with a weaker base, any sort of event could carry the title 'All England'. The headline 'All England' sounded a lot more important than 'Cobridge track championship'. Sixteen of the best drivers were booked to appear on Saturday 22 July but, just like the meeting two weeks before, this event too had to be cancelled due to heavy rain. In fact, July 1939 was to be the wettest July for seventeen years; in all, 7.1in of rain fell on Stoke-on-Trent that month. The 'All England Championship', like the previous Coventry match had to be put back another week and rescheduled for Saturday 29 July. Once again this date too proved to be a disaster, on that day alone 1.02in of rain fell on the city, every outdoor and sporting event had to be cancelled, it was the wettest day of the month. There were only six days throughout July 1939 when it didn't rain in Stoke-on-Trent!

It was not only Cobridge that was suffering from the vagaries of the English summer. The only other track staging full time midget car racing, Coventry, was also having problems weather-wise. After their opening meeting early in April they had continued presenting car meetings on a more or less fortnightly basis. After a three-week break in late June, due to a rained-off meeting and the annual Coventry holidays, they reverted to their traditional weekly meetings. The first two Sundays of July – the second and ninth – went well, but after that the next three Sunday meetings were called off. 'Flooding everywhere', 'More Summer Flooding' and 'Extensive Storm Damage' were the leading stories of the Coventry newspapers. Racing at Brandon never recovered from this break in continuity due to the weather and midget car racing faded away there. In fact motorcycle speedway was set to return there in September.

Back at Stoke it was now the Potters Wakes Week with all the Pottery factories closed down for two weeks. The new month of August might bring with it better luck with the weather. To coincide with the holidays, a change of race night was decided. Instead of re-running the meeting on Saturday 5 August, the event was brought forward to Thursday 3 August. With the motorcycle speedway at Sun Street now defunct, Thursday's race night should attract the 'floating' spectator. The weather forecast for that day was bright intervals and showers – whether this meeting took place is not known. Despite extensive searches of extant material, nothing, so far, has come to light. Neither is there any reference to a proposed meeting on or around 25 August when Cobridge Tigers were to race against a side called Brandon. The newspapers and Media of the time had far more important events to write about. On the same day that the advert appeared for the Brandon match the newspaper headlines ominously stated 'Imminent Peril of War'. By the following week, war had been declared and all sporting activities immediately ceased.

An interesting motor racing interlude had come to an end. The track and facilities were, at the time, perfect for midget car speedway, the large track and wide sweeping bends were ideal. The track surface could have been perfected and developed especially for the cars instead of having to make compromises for the speedway bike racers.

eight

Conclusion

When the war ended and motor sport slowly returned, there was no place for car racing at either of the Potteries stadiums. Greyhound racing flourished and a boom period was witnessed at both arenas. As the country tried to rebuild, the population that had been starved of entertainment flooded back to sporting events. This was a golden age for outdoor sporting activities and huge crowds flocked to all manner of sporting venues. Motor racing was to draw vast crowds but unfortunately, midget car fans were starved of their branch of motor racing. This sport did continue but on a very limited basis compared to 1938/39. There was one further concerted effort to establish midget car racing in Britain. In 1948 twenty American midget car drivers, together with their cars and equipment, descended on London. This invasion was masterminded by H.J. 'Bob' Topping, a wealthy Californian business tycoon and avid midget car fan. At tracks especially constructed around the soccer pitches of Chelsea's Stamford Bridge and Charlton's Valley Stadium together with Walthamstow's greyhound stadium. The cars looked fantastic, the publicity well-oiled, and the drivers colourful and professional. Yet after just five weeks, the troupe returned home. Crowds of 50,000 watched the first meeting at Stamford Bridge followed by a further 25,000 at Walthamstow. The following week there was less than half that amount; the spectators then just drifted away. A major cause of this decline was the negative reporting of the English Press who, after witnessing the first meetings, encouraged people to stay away! They came up with such headlines as 'Dodge em'. The troupe was not given enough time to iron out the teething problems that occurred, the primary one being the poor racing surface and narrowness of the circuits. The American midget cars were just not allowed to show off how good they were. It was like driving a Grand Prix car around a rough and bumpy go-kart track.

The people of Stoke who were looking for the thrills of motorised sport switch-ed their allegiance to motorcycle speedway racing. Sun Street re-opened for motorcycle speedway in 1947 and ran successfully until 1953 when, as with most spectator sports, firstly entertainment tax and then the popularity of television caused a decline in evening entertainment. A form of car racing did make a comeback to Sun Street in 1954 when a few Stock Car meetings were held there that year. Six years later, a national revival in the fortunes of motorcycle speedway saw this sport re-introduced for a further four years. When Sun Street finally closed in 1963 the stadium and surrounding land was sold off for light industrial development. The stadium at Cobridge never did see the return of motor sport; the cinder track was used for athletics by the local clubs and schools until a new purpose-built athletics track was constructed in the City. There were always rumours that the track would be re-used for motor sport, both two-wheeled and four, but nothing ever came of these proposals, mainly because of environmental issues. The Albion Stadium went the same way as Sun Street, closing down in the 1980s to make way for housing development.

In the late 1940s, drivers that had thrilled the locals had moved on to other things. Some, like Gene Crowley and Les White, were part of a small group that tried to revive the sport after the war. They had nothing to do with the Toppings' abortive attempt to introduce US midget racing, but briefly joined forces with Dave Hughes, of Northampton, who brought up as many Skirrow Specials as he could and toured the UK with his small group of drivers. Ironically, one of their last races was at Coventry in 1958 with just five cars. Locally, nothing was heard of Reg Grice. Of the other North Staffordshire drivers, all but one took no further part in motor racing. Les Foster remained for a while connected with the motor trade, becoming an auctioneer at several local car sales before moving to Chester where he became involved in horse racing. Hal Palfyrman hung on to his car for a short while after the war, keeping it in a shed on an allotment in the Northwood area of the Potteries where he would occasionally start up the car to the annoyance of the neighbours! The car was eventually sold on to an unknown buyer. Hal did not continue his association with the motoring world but built up one of the Potteries' most successful electrical contractors, a company that still exists today.

Garage owner and promoter Cecil Heath did continue racing after the war. He owned and raced several cars at both hill-climbs and race meetings. He built his own car (the 'Heath Special') which he fitted with a J.A.P. engine. Later he moved on to a Cooper 1100 and XK120 Jaguar, which he raced and rallied, taking part not only in the R.A.C. rally but also once in the Monte Carlo rally. He also raced the Jaguar in the long distance Goodwood Nine Hour Race. The Station Garage that he founded is now a Honda dealership.

Although not a permanent success, the brief interlude of midget car speedway did give the people of the Potteries a chance to witness single-seater motor racing at close quarters. The sport did try to establish itself in this country but why it did not succeed is subject to conjecture. Perhaps it was trying to emulate motorcycle speedway racing too much. Often sharing the same stadiums did not help. There was always going to be a conflict of interest; when all is said and done, it was down to finances. The speedway bikes provided faster and closer racing. This sport was well established and riders well rewarded too, so any threat to the riders' livelihood was stamped on. Some speedway riders did hedge their bets and try car speedway, perhaps, just in case cars became more popular, but more than likely they were curious about all things mechanical. Four wheels and two wheels somehow never mixed on the loose cinder tracks of this country. By trying to follow the bike formula of four cars per race and team events, it forced spectators to directly compare the midget cars with the speedway bikes. In Australia and the USA, it was the individual events that pulled in the crowds with as many cars on the track as possible. This format had been tried in the second half of team matches and had proved very popular with the spectators. The fault of midget car speedway to establish itself lay more than anything with its too close a comparison with the speedway bikes. Both sports drew their fan base from well-populated urban areas and both were vying for the same audience. Hindsight suggests that a track filled with cars jockeying and dicing for position would have proved a more thrilling spectacle than team racing. When motorcycle speedway lost its monopoly on the small dirt ovals to stock-car racing in the mid-1950s it was the thrill of seeing lots of cars on the track and over distances longer than four laps that drew in the spectators – that is, from a racing point of view as opposed to the crashing and smashing viewpoint. At that time, in the late 1930s, midget car speedway was a new form of motor sport and had no precedent to follow and, therefore, it was natural to copy the speedway bikes. Just as the early motoring events at Brooklands aped horse race meetings, with driver's colours, betting and handicaps, so midget cars aped motorcycle speedway rather than set its own agenda. It had taken midget

Modern-day midgets are alive and well. Eric Walker in a Westfield. (Courtesy of Eric Walker)

car builders far too long to construct decent machines for the dirt tracks. Suitable cars had been at least six or seven years in development before the right formula was found, whereas the bikes had the right set up much quicker. The early cars had been slow, cumbersome, and unreliable; but by the time cars were suitably developed, circumstances had played into the hands of the motorcycle speedway promoters and riders. It had proved too difficult to fight back. Coventry and Hanley had been the jewel in the crown of midget car speedway racing. Without the influence of the two-wheeled brigade, both tracks were able to set their own agendas.

Nowadays, in this country, all sorts of cars take to the short circuit ovals, from BRISCA F1 stock-cars down to banger racing. Single-seater cars still compete on the ovals under the guise of Grand Prix midget cars. Although stadiums are not able to run meetings solely for single-seater midget cars, there are sufficient cars around to compete in 'mixed meetings' and hold their own championship.

Acknowledgements

I n compiling this book I would like to thank a whole host of people without whose assistance, unselfishness and encouragement, this work would not have been written. Firstly, my daughters Elizabeth and Victoria – along with her husband Lee, who patiently guided me through the complexities of information technology and downloaded many photographs that fellow enthusiasts had sent me. Secondly, friends Duncan and Susan Williams, Susan for her typing and Duncan for accompanying me on several trips up and down the country collating information. Many speedway historians and collectors have been extremely generous in allowing me to copy items and articles from their archives and collections. The Scottish connection has been very active in their support. Jim Henry's, Graham Frazer's and Ian Sommerville's contributions have proved invaluable. Other historians and collectors who have supplied information were Colin Parker, Barry Stevenson, Trevor James, John Pearson, Alan Jones, Dave Stone, Peter Halton, Vic Butcher, Adrian Pavey, John Jervis, Adrian Weltch, Denis Jones, Graham Brown, Martin Dodswell, Norman Jacobs and Bryan Tungate. There were also several specialists who contributed including J.A.P. engine experts Jeff Clew, Gordon Dobbie, Ian Patterson, Denis Rushton and Terry Wright. Amongst the motoring fraternity who assisted were John Maddison, Mark Joseland, members of staff at the library of the V.S.C.C., the National Motor Museum at Beaulieu and James Peacop of Mouldsworth Motor Museum, Cheshire. I am also indebted to midget car specialists Andy Abrahams, Eric Walker and John Hyam. The overseas contributors need singling out too, and if it hadn't been for Gerald Santibanes in the USA and the Australian stalwarts Brian Darby, Kevin Emmerson, Garry Baker and Bill Lawler, much of their Continents' history could not have been included. My grateful thanks for supplying certain photographs go to Bob Light,

John Abberly of 'The Sentinal', Peter Haines and the late Dave Gahndi. My special thanks goes to the relatives of former drivers, namely Malcolm Skirrow, Brian Heath, Peter and John Palyfryman, Gina Proctor, Nicholas Hanstock, Brian deMattos, Rod Pashley, Harry Marsh, Malcolm White and most importantly Roy Chiswell. I would also like to thank the staff at my local library in Newcastle-under-Lyme, particularly Paul, Brian and June. Individual thanks go to Noel Clark, John Ogden and Don Gray for their encouragement and persistence in ferreting out articles from obscure magazines. Lastly but not least, many thanks go to those who have helped with improving photographs; Mike Salt, Jim Mellenchip and Mark McAdams.

Other titles published by Tempus

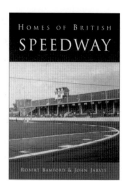

Homes of British Speedway

ROBERT BAMFORD AND JOHN JARVIS

Having arrived in Britain in the late 1920s, dirt-track racing soon established itself as an incredibly popular national sport. By the end of 1928, there were over fifty tracks throughout Britain. Many venues were opened and run sporadically over the next seven decades, particularly during the heyday of speedway after the Second World War when interest was phenomenally high.

This book features over 300 venues throughout Britain and will be of interest to an fan of the shale game.

0 7524 2210 3

Stoke City Football Club

TONY MATTHEWS

As founder members of the Football League, Stoke City Football Club has a long and proud tradition. This book illustrated their impressive history with over 200 high-quality images, including old team groups, action shots, player portraits and programm covers. This book is an essential read for anyone with an interest in Stoke City. Older fans will take enormous pleasure from seeing the events and players they remember, while younger supporters get a fascinating glimpse of this club's fine sporting heritage

0 7524 1698 7

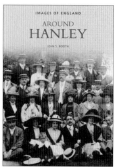

Around Hanley

JOHN BOOTH

This fascinating collection of photographs illustrates life as it was in the rapidly developing pottery town of Hanley. Originally just a single farm, Hanley grew into the largest and most central town in the greater area of Stoke-on-Trent, blossoming in the early twentie century with the development of heavy industry. This visual history reflects the town as it was at that time, the height of its successes. John Booth's nostalgic presentation provides an insight into the history and characters of Hanley, home of the famous Wedgwood potter works and birthplace of legendary footballer Sir Stanley Matthews.

0 7524 3407 1

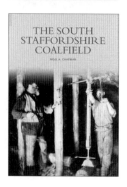

South Staffordshire Collieries

NIGEL CHAPMAN

At one time, South Staffordshire had the finest bed of coal that had ever been discovered. This book relates the history of the long-gone Black Country collieries that flourished in the age of the Industrial Revolution, and which did a lot to create the West Midlands that exists today. Over 200 old photographs illustrate the working conditions and the men who were employed in the collieries.

0 7524 3102 1

If you are interested in purchasing other books published by Tempus, or in case you have difficulty finding any Tempus books in your local bookshop, you can also place orders directly through our website

www.tempus-publishing.com